SY 0096812 9

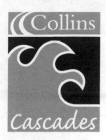

As it Happens

ED. ROSY BORDER

Cascades consultants:
John Mannion, former Head of English, London
Sheena Davies, Principal Teacher of English, Glasgow
Adrian Jackson, General English Advisor, West Sussex
Geoff Fox, Lecturer at the University of Exeter School of
    Education, and a National Curriculum Advisor
Emily Rought-Brooks, Head of English, London
Antonia Sharpe, English teacher, London

ED. ROSY BORDER

As it Happens

Collins

An imprint of HarperCollins*Publishers*

Published by HarperCollins*Publishers*,
77–85 Fulham Palace Rd, London W6 8JB

Selection © Rosy Border 2001

ISBN 000 711 364–1

First published in Great Britain by HarperCollins*Publishers* 2001

The right of Rosy Border to be identified as the editor of this work is
asserted.

With thanks to John Mannion.

British Library Cataloguing in Publication Data
A catalogue record for this book is available from the British Library.

Cover design by Ken Vail Graphic Design, Cambridge
Cover photograph by PA Photos
Printed and bound in Hong Kong
Commissioned by Thomas Allain-Chapman
Edited by Gaynor Spry
Production by Katie Morris

Contents

---

* pre-1914 texts

---

* pre-1914 texts
† diary

* pre-1914 texts

Introduction

What is reportage? One English dictionary defines it as 'journalistic reporting'; another says it is 'reported matter; gossip'. Look in a French dictionary, however, and you will find *reportage* defined as '(live) commentary' or 'coverage'. *Le grand reportage* is defined as 'coverage of important events'. So if a modest wedding, a minor court case and a village football match qualify as *reportage*, a royal wedding, a murder trial and a Cup Final will probably belong in the *grand reportage* section. First-hand reports of epoch-making events like Neil Armstrong's moon walk in 1969 ('That's one small step for man, one giant leap for mankind') are about as *grand* as you can get.

Reportage is not quite the same as journalism, although every newspaper or magazine contains some reportage. In the daily editorial of *The Times* a senior reporter comments on an item of news. To do this he or she has probably had to read several different reports, each treating the same topic in a different way. On the other hand, *The Times's* Parliamentary page is pure reportage. Someone sits in the gallery taking notes: what went on in the Chamber, who said what and to whom, and what the consequences were. The novelist Charles Dickens was a Parliamentary correspondent in his time, and produced very readable and funny reports.

Reportage is not the same as history either, although all historians draw on reportage as part of their source material. A history book is like a patchwork quilt. An individual piece may be exciting, beautiful or fascinating in its own right, but the quiltmaker/historian has chosen it less for its own qualities than for the contribution it can make to the whole picture. One eyewitness account does not make a history of the Napoleonic Wars, or even of the Battle of the Nile. But John Nichol's story (see page 40) is an excellent piece of reportage in its own right. It begs a lot of questions – what were women and children doing on board a warship? Did Nichol, who lived in an age when relatively few people could read and write, write the report himself? We might go hunting for answers, but that would take us away from reportage and into historical research.

So what does reportage do? It takes the word 'live' out of brackets in '(live) commentary'. All true reportage has an element of 'I was there'. 'There' could be the surface of the moon, the North-West frontier, a deathbed, or an interview with someone either rivetingly interesting or so dull as to be different. The narrator could be describing events that happened this morning in a diary, or recalling those of fifty years ago in a memoir; it is the element of being there that matters, just as with travel writing.

Finding reports from people who were 'there' becomes harder the further back in history we go. This is not at all surprising; for a long time illiteracy was the norm. Printing did not reach the western world until the late Middle Ages and, in the western world at least, books were copied by hand.

Books get damaged or destroyed: wholesale, as in the deliberate burning of the great library in Alexandria, or piecemeal, as in the practice of scraping the ink off old manuscripts so that other texts could be written on them. Luckily for us, some important old material survived the scraping process and could be read underneath the new writing. It is not surprising that so few very early accounts have come down to us over the centuries.

Much reportage comes from diaries. The problem here is that dramatic things happen to dull people as well as to interesting ones. On 14 July 1789, on the day the French Revolution broke out, King Louis XVI of France apparently wrote in his diary, 'Rien' – 'Nothing to report'. He was wrong, and you can read about his execution on page 104. Queen Victoria's *Our Life in the Highlands*, though a bestseller in its time, makes tame reading today.

It would, however, be wrong to blame either Louis or Victoria for dullness. Diarists usually write not for posterity but for themselves. Queen Victoria in particular comes over as a homely little body, devoted to her family. Her diary and sketches record whatever interested her, including her servants, a subject few great ladies of her time concerned themselves with.

Not all diaries are dull, however. Superb reports on the Great Plague of the fourteenth century (see page 86) and Great Fire of London (see page 95) come from the seventeenth-century diarist Samuel Pepys. Editing Pepys's diary for an anthology like this involves weeding out accounts of financial transactions, dinner parties and adventures with his mistresses, but it is worth the trouble. Pepys at his best can make an everyday event as exciting as the Battle of Trafalgar, but with endearing personal touches. People may be dying like flies all around, but life goes on. So it is probably true to say that the best reportage often combines the momentous with the mundane.

For thousands of years reportage depended on the ability to paint pictures with words. Suetonius's pen portraits of the Roman emperors rely entirely on his skill with language. His description of Nero's ambitions as a performer (see page 74) conjures up a vain and vainglorious emperor with little sense of the limits of his talents.

When newspapers and magazines became common, editors would often commission artists to illustrate a particularly dramatic report. The pictures always played a secondary role: without the words they were mere decoration. In the same way, photography, film and sound recording have not harmed reportage as an art form. Rather, they have encouraged new skills. It takes talent to write a script which will pull together a mass of recorded sound and pictures into a meaningful whole.

If a television report is to be good, we should be able to listen to it while doing something else: the pictures merely confirm what the words have already conveyed. It does not matter if you have never seen Fergal Keane's Rwanda reports on television. Read a page or two of 'Genocide in Rwanda' (see page 130), close your eyes and you are there. Reportage is alive and well in the twenty-first century.

Signs of the Times

A good eyewitness account is like a narrow beam of light in a dark room. Enough eyewitness accounts enable the historian to cast light on the whole scene, make sense of it and write something meaningful about it. All the events in this section shed light on historic events: the first landing on the Moon in 1969, the fall of the infamous Marcos regime in the Philippines in 1986, and finally the toppling of the Serb tyrant Slobodan Milosovic in 2000.

NASA selected its astronauts for skills other than their creative writing. All the same, their reports are priceless: how many people have seen the Moon by earthlight, or experienced the effects of her low gravity?

The other two pieces were written by experienced journalists. They knew how to show the broad picture, then shine their torches on the details that bring the scene to life: the monogrammed towels in Manila, the Serbian policemen abandoning their riot gear and joining the crowd in their celebration.

All three pieces will be important to historians in the future: meanwhile, enjoy them today!

The First Men on the Moon

Neil Armstrong and Edwin ('Buzz') Aldrin

On 16 July 1969 Apollo 11 was launched. Three men were on board: Michael Collins, Neil Armstrong and Edwin ('Buzz') Aldrin. At 3.56 am, British Summer Time, on 21 July 1969, Armstrong stepped off the ladder of the lunar landing vehicle Eagle onto the surface of the moon. Aldrin joined him, while Collins manned the main spacecraft. These men were not journalists. They were astronauts: supremely fit Air Force officers with science degrees and the right attitude. A journalist might have sent back a more exciting report, but NASA was not in the business of exciting reportage. Theirs was an information-gathering exercise. Apollo 11 contained sophisticated instruments which worked non-stop, gathering and processing data. The information they brought back kept scientists busy for years.

Armstrong: Of all the spectacular views we had, the most impressive to me was on the way to the moon, when we flew through its shadow. We were still thousands of miles away, but close enough so that the moon almost filled our circular window. It was eclipsing the sun, from our position, and the corona of the sun[1] was visible around the limb of the moon as a gigantic lens-shaped or saucer-shaped light, stretching out to several lunar diameters. That was magnificent, but the moon was even more so. We were in its shadow, so there was no part of it illuminated by the sun. It was illuminated only by earthshine ...

Aldrin: The moon was a very natural and pleasant environment in which to work. It had many of the advantages of zero gravity, but it was in a sense less *lonesome* than Zero G, where you always have to pay attention to securing attachment points to give you some sort of leverage ... As we deployed our experiments on the surface we had to jettison[2] things like

---

[1] **corona of the sun:** circle of light round the sun
[2] **jettison:** throw away

remains of a box of monogrammed towels. We realised they had Imelda's initials. There were a couple left. They were irresistible.

I couldn't believe I would be able to find the actual Marcos apartments, and I knew there was no point in asking. We went up some servants' stairs, at the foot of which I remember seeing an opened crate with two large green jade plates. They were so large as to be vulgar. On the first floor a door opened, and we found ourselves in the great hall where the press conferences had been held. This was the one bit of the palace the crowd would recognise, as it had so often watched Marcos being televised from here. People ran and sat on his throne and began giving mock press conferences, issuing orders in his deep voice, falling about with laughter or just gaping at the splendour of the room. It was all fully lit. Nobody had bothered, as they left, to turn out the lights.

I remembered that the first time I had been here, the day after the election, Imelda had slipped in and sat at the side. She must have come from that direction. I went to investigate.

And now, for a short while, I was away from the crowd with just one other person, a shy and absolutely thunderstruck Filipino. We had found our way, we realised, into the Marcoses' private rooms. There was a library, and my companion gazed in wonder at the leather-bound volumes while I admired the collection of art books all carefully catalogued and with their numbers on the spines. This was the reference library for Imelda's worldwide collection of treasures. She must have thumbed through them thinking: *I'd like one of them,* or *I've got a couple of them in New York,* or *That's in our London house.* And then there was the Blue Drawing Room with its twin portraits of the Marcoses, where I simply remember standing with my companion and saying, 'It's beautiful, isn't it.' It wasn't that it *was* beautiful. It looked as if it had been purchased at Harrods. It was just that, after all the crowds and riots, we had landed up in this peaceful, luxurious den. My companion had never seen anything like it. He didn't take anything. He hardly dared touch the furnishings and trinkets. We both simply could not believe that we were there and the Marcoses weren't.

I wish I could remember it all better. For instance, it seemed to me that in every room I saw, practically on every available surface, there was a signed photograph of Nancy Reagan. But this can hardly be literally true. It just felt as if there was a lot of Nancy in evidence. Another of the rooms had a grand piano. I sat down. 'Can you play?' said my companion.

'A little,' I exaggerated. I can play Bach's Prelude in C, and this is what I proceeded to do, but my companion had obviously hoped for something more racy.

A soldier came in, carrying a rifle. 'Please co-operate,' he said. The soldier looked just as overawed by the place as we were. We co-operated.

When I returned down the service stairs, I noticed that the green jade plates were gone, but there was still some Evian water to be had. I was very thirsty, as it happened. But the revolution had asked me to co-operate. So I did.

Outside, the awe had communicated itself to several members of the crowd. They stood by the fountain looking down at the coloured lights beneath the water, not saying anything. I went to the parapet[6] and looked across the river. I thought: somebody's still fighting; there are still some loyal troops. Then I thought: that's crazy – they can't have started fighting now. I realised that I was back in Saigon yet again. *There* indeed there had been fighting on the other side of the river. But here it was fireworks. The whole city was celebrating.

---

[6] **parapet:** low wall along the edge of the balcony

Good Evening, Liberated Serbia

Misha Glenny

In September 2000 there were elections in Serbia. Slobodan Milosevic was voted out of power after a 13-year reign of terror and violence. At first he refused to concede defeat and demanded a recount. Eventually he accepted the inevitable and, like many defeated British politicians, he told interviewers that he welcomed the chance to spend more time with his family. As he was wanted for war crimes he seemed unlikely to get his wish. And the people made their feelings clear – his time of power was over.

Slobodan Milosevic's state was burning to the ground last night as a million people seized Belgrade in a ferocious outburst of revolutionary power.

The federal parliament went up in flames in the early afternoon before a vast crowd stormed Radio Television Serbia, a hated symbol of Mr Milosevic's regime, and turned it into a blaze that spewed thick black smoke across the city centre.

By mid-evening, Serbs from across the country were celebrating in a joyous hysteria as Vojislav Kostunica, the Opposition leader who claimed victory in last month's presidential election, told them: 'Good evening, liberated Serbia'. A Serbian revolution had begun.

'We are living in the last twitches of Milosevic's regime,' Mr Kostunica told the crowd, 'Democracy has happened in Serbia. Communism is falling. It is just a matter of hours.' He later got straight down to business, calling an emergency session of both houses of parliament.

Late yesterday evening there were reports that Mr Milosevic had fled by helicopter and plane to Moscow; that three Antonovs[1] had taken off from a military air base near Belgrade; that he was in a bunker; that the SAS were sending a snatch squad to arrest him. Whichever, if any, was

---

[1] ***Antonovs:*** Russian-built warplanes (named after their designer, Oleg Antonov)

true, there was no doubt on the ground that his 13-year rule was over. A laughing Opposition leader, Dragoljub Micunovic, told me: 'He's finished. There's no way back for him now.'

Parliament was torched at the very start of the mass demonstration. Police launched dozens of teargas canisters into the crowd, but demonstrators on the steps of the parliament responded by charging into the building, led by Cedomir Jovanovic, a leading member of the Opposition.

'We just went for it,' he told me with a broad, victorious smile on his face. 'We took the parliament.' Young men armed with rods and sticks began sacking the building, smashing windows, trampling on typewriters and telephones and burning pictures of Slobodan Milosevic.

In scenes unprecedented even in the troubled Balkans, groups of youths armed with improvised weapons were roaming the city, smashing anything associated with the Government. Members of the Resistance movement seized the old offices of the independent Radio B92, and broadcast victory messages.

Students and workers went on to occupy all the main media centres. At seven o'clock, they seized TV Serbia's second studio in the suburb of Kostunik and began broadcasting 'Freedom Television'.

Battling through a poisonous fog of teargas that hung over the city for most of the afternoon, the crowd reformed again and again to take complete control of the city. Police vehicles were overturned, smashed and set on fire and by six o'clock the entire police force had retreated to its stations. Terrified officers handed their shields and batons to the demonstrators and promised never again to move against the people. [Later many were seen drinking and celebrating with the protesters.]

In [a street] in old Belgrade, I watched as police fled for their lives as the mob forced its way into the [police sation] and began ripping apart everything in sight. Even 70 members of the Unit of Special Operations stripped off their uniform, helmets and weapons and left them for the crowd to gather up.

All day, the city was ringing with the deafening roar of a million people singing this revolution's hymn: 'Slobodan, Slobodan, Save Serbia, Kill Yourself.'

By nightfall Belgrade had been transformed into the biggest party Serbia had seen as people sang and danced in the streets to folk music blasting out of loudspeakers.

'This is the end of ten years of darkness and the start of a new Serbia,' a woman of 80 told me in tears.

'The nightmare's over. He's finished! He's finished,' a delirious[2] 25-year-old student shouted.

The people of Serbia look to have brought to an end one of the most despised men in recent European history.

---

[2] ***delirious:*** wildly excited

Activities

Understanding
The First Men on the Moon
1 Reread Neil Armstrong's description carefully and draw a diagram of the relative positions of the spaceship, the Moon, the Sun and the Earth.
2 State briefly the aspects of the moon that impressed Armstrong and Aldrin.

The Fall of President Marcos
3 The dismissal of a dictator from power is a hugely significant event from the point of view of the people who have been oppressed, but the actual process itself might seem confused and nonsensical from the point of view of those actually present. Find quotations from the extract that reflect the importance of the decisions being made, and also quotations that reflect the absurdity of the events.
4 Reread the description of President Marcos's press conference. What were the issues at stake?
5 What can you infer about the lifestyle of President Marcos and his family from this description?

Good Evening, Liberated Serbia
6 What was the first sign that Milosevic could no longer stay in power?
7 How does Misha Glenny try to give an impression of the scale of the events being described?

Style
The First Men on the Moon
8 Armstrong and Aldrin were both trained as scientists and tend to focus on facts rather than emotions. How do the two men express their emotions in these extracts?
9 Aldrin uses the word 'lonesome' to describe working in zero gravity. What word do you think he would have used if he had been English rather than American?

The Fall of President Marcos
10 Reread the section describing the Marcos's library. James Fenton does not state how he feels about Imelda Marcos but what does this section reveal about the sort of woman she was? Think about why Fenton selects certain items for description and the kind of attitude that a collector of such objects might have.
11 What are the advantages and disadvantages of the first person narrative style that Fenton has used in his article?

Good Evening, Liberated Serbia

12 Identify the adjectives and adverbials in Misha Glenny's description in the second paragraph. How do these words and phrases make the description more powerful?

13 ▷ Look again at the quotations that Glenny has used. Some might have been spoken in English but most will be translations. With a partner, discuss whether the quotations sound like words actually spoken, or whether they have been 'tidied up'.

14 How does Glenny try to give the descriptions of the events a more intimate, human perspective?

15 Prepare the script for a television news report of these events. Would you use all Glenny's text or would you let pictures and images tell more of the story? Would you use more or less quotation from eyewitnesses?

Speaking and listening

16 ▷ Choose one of the events described in this section and improvise a dialogue between two people involved. Think about what you might be doing, such as piloting a moon rocket or storming a television station, as well as what you would be saying.

17 ▷ Describe a 'great event' that you have attended to a partner. It could be something personal like a wedding or it could be a large occasion like a football match or a concert.

Comparisons

18 Of the three extracts, which do you think reveals the most about the person who wrote it? Give reasons for your answer.

19 All three extracts show ordinary human emotions in the context of momentous and important events. How well does each extract help you to imagine what it would have been like to have been present at the event?

Further activity

20 Choose a 'great event' from history, research it and describe it from your own personal point of view. You might be one of the principal characters like Armstrong and Aldrin or you might be a reporter like James Fenton or Misha Glenny.

All in a Day's Work

Today 'oral history' is very fashionable. Researchers take down the reminiscences of the people they meet and record them for future generations. Many such interviews deal with people whose jobs seem bizarre to us in twenty-first-century Britain. When, for example, did you last meet a 'pure finder', who sold dog dirt to the tannery to cure leather?

There are many harrowing reports of working conditions of the past – three of those reports are included here. We can all feel thankful that, at least in the developed world, working conditions have improved hugely since the days when young girls toiled for 20p a week in a match factory. You will no longer find children working down coal mines in the USA, or indeed sticking labels on jars in rat-infested London warehouses. The chocolate factory in Frank Johnson's description is noisy, yes; but its staff work reasonable hours in conscientiously inspected surroundings for an agreed rate of pay. They all have contracts of employment setting down their duties, responsibilities and rights; and they are protected from exploitation by employment legislation.

But we do not need to travel back in time to experience the terrible working conditions of the past. There is very little employment legislation to protect workers in developing countries. Children still toil in factories and down mines. To read William Dalrymple's description of the shoe factory in Aleppo is to glimpse a world where profit rules and the weak and helpless serve.

Match Girls

Annie Besant

Annie Besant campaigned for improved working conditions for the girls who made matches in Bryant and May's London factory. This 1888 article led to a boycott of[1] Bryant and May's matches and then to successful industrial action.

The hour for commencing work is half-past six in summer and eight in winter; work concludes at six pm. Half an hour is allowed for breakfast and an hour for dinner. This long day of work is performed by young girls, who have to stand the whole of the time. A typical case is that of a girl of sixteen, a piece-worker;[2] she earns 4 shillings[3] a week, and lives with a sister, employed by the same firm, who 'earns good money, as much as 8 or 9 shillings per week'. Out of the earnings 2 shillings is paid for the rent of one room; the child lives only on bread and butter and tea, alike for breakfast and dinner, but related with dancing eyes that once a month she went to a meal where 'you get coffee, and bread and butter, and jam, and marmalade, and lots of it' ...

The splendid salary of 4 shillings is subject to deductions in the shape of fines; if the feet are dirty, or the ground under the bench is left untidy, a fine of 3d[4] is inflicted; for putting 'burnts' – matches that have caught fire during the work – on the bench, 1 shilling has been forfeited, and one unhappy girl was once fined 2 shillings and sixpence for some unknown crime. If a girl leaves four or five matches on her bench when she goes for a fresh 'frame', she is fined 3d, and in some departments a fine of 3d is inflicted for talking ... One girl was fined a shilling for letting the web twist around a machine in the endeavour to save her fingers from being cut, and was sharply told to take care of the machine, 'never mind your fingers'. Another, who

---

[1] **boycott of:** refusal to buy
[2] **piece-worker:** worker paid for the amount of pieces of work she/he completes
[3] **4 shillings:** 20p
[4] **3d:** three old pennies

carried out the instructions and lost a finger thereby, was left unsupported while she was helpless.

A very bitter memory survives in the factory. Mr Theodore Bryant, to show his admiration of Mr Gladstone and the greatness of his own public spirit, bethought him to erect a statue to that eminent[5] statesman. In order that his workgirls might have the privilege of contributing, he stopped a shilling each out of their wages, and further deprived them of half-a-day's work by closing the factory, 'giving them a holiday'. ('We don't want no holidays,' said one of the girls pathetically for – needless to say – the poorer employees of such a firm lose their wages when a holiday is 'given'.) So furious were the girls at this cruel plundering, that many went to the unveiling of the statue with stones and bricks in their pockets, and I was conscious of a wish that some of those bricks had made an impression on Mr Bryant's conscience. Later on they surrounded the statue – 'we paid for it' they cried savagely – shouting and yelling, and a gruesome story is told that some cut their arms and let their blood trickle on the marble paid for, in very truth, by their blood ...

With chattel slaves Mr Bryant could not have made his huge fortune, for he could not have fed, clothed and housed them for 4 shillings a week each, and they would have had a definite money value which would have served as a protection. But who cares for the fate of these white wage slaves? Born in slums, driven to work while still children, undersized because underfed, oppressed because helpless, flung aside as soon as worked out, who cares if they die or go on the streets, provided the Bryant and May shareholders get their 23 per cent and Mr Theodore Bryant can erect statues and buy parks? Oh if we had but a people's Dante,[6] to make a special circle in the Inferno for those who live on this misery, and suck wealth out of the starvation of helpless girls.

Failing a poet ... let us at least avoid being 'partakers of their sins' by abstaining from using their commodities.

---

[5] **eminent:** distinguished
[6] **Dante:** author of 'The Divine Comedy', a poem about hell

Sixteen Ton

Studs Terkel

'Sixteen ton, and what do you get?
Another day over and deeper in debt.
Saint Peter, don't you call me, 'cos I can't go –
I owe my soul to the company store.'

The 'Depression' in the USA was a period of mass unemployment which lasted from the time of the Wall Street Crash in 1929 until the beginning of the Second World War in 1939. Hard Times is Studs Terkel's collection of first-hand reports about those years. Here Buddy Blankenship talks about his time as a coal miner.

We lived eight miles from the mine, and we had to ride it horseback. I was riding behind my dad. Many times I'd have to git off and hammer his feet out of the stirrups. They'd be froze in the stirrups. It was cold, you know. When you came out of the mines, your feet would be wet of sweat and wet where you were walking on the bottom. And get up on those steel stirrups, while you're riding eight miles, your feet'd be frozen and you couldn't get 'em out of the stirrups. I'd have to hammer 'em out. His feet were numb, and they wouldn't hurt till they started to get warm, and then they would get to hurting.

We got up at five in the morning, start at six. We got out at ten that night. We'd work about sixteen hours a day, seventeen hours. The boss said we had to clean up. If we didn't clean up, next morning there'd be another man in the mine to clean it up. The motor man would say: 'How many cars you got? Five more. Well, hurry up, we want to get out of here.'

They was gettin' a dollar seventy-five a day. We'd get sixty to sixty-five ton a day – that is, both us, me and Dad. Then they changed me off and let me get a dollar and a half a day. I was trappin'.

Trappin'? The trap door was shut so the air would circulate through the mine. Then the motor come along, I'd open it up. I had to stay there till everybody quit. Then we'd walk about two miles and a half till we got outside. We walked about a mile before we got to where we could get our horses. We got down to the horses, why we rode about eight miles before we got to home. Summertimes it wasn't too bad. But wintertimes, boy, it was rough. You'd get snowbound and it would get so you couldn't get in and out. Ice'd be so bad ... an' dangerous. Of course, we had to go to work. We didn't eat if we didn't go.

About '32, it got so they wouldn't let us work but two days a week. We saved $20 in the office. They laid us off two weeks till we traded that $20 in the store. We had to trade it out in the store, or we didn't get to work no more. What we made, we had to go next evening and trade it off. They didn't let you draw no money at all. It was scrip.[1] They had a man top of the hill who took your tonnage down, how many tons you loaded, and it was sent up to the scrip office. If you made $20 over your expenses – for house, rent, lights and all[2] – why, then they laid you off till you spent that $20.

---

[1] **scrip:** certificates issued by the employer instead of money
[2] (the workers' houses belonged to the company too)

A Blacking Warehouse in the 1820s

Charles Dickens

When Charles Dickens was 12 his father lost his job and Charles had to go to work in a factory which made blacking,[1] interrupting his education. Mr Dickens, who served time in a debtors' prison, was the model for Mr Micawber in Charles's novel David Copperfield. *Later, when the family fortunes improved, Charles was able to continue his education, to the great benefit of English literature.*

James Lambert, a relative, knowing what our domestic circumstances then were, proposed that I should go into a blacking warehouse, to be as useful as I could, at a salary of six shillings[2] a week ... The offer was accepted very willingly by my father and mother, and on a Monday morning I went down to the blacking warehouse to begin my business life.

The blacking warehouse was a crazy, tumble-down old house, abutting of course on the river, and literally overrun with rats. Its wainscoted[3] rooms and its rotten floors and staircase, with the old grey rats swarming down in the cellars, and the sound of their squeaking and scuffling coming up the stairs at all times, and the dirt and decay of the place, rise up visibly before me as if I were there again. The counting-house was on the first floor, looking over the coal-barges on the river. There was a recess in it, in which I was to sit and work. My work was to cover the pots of paste-blacking, first with a piece of oil-paper and then with a piece of blue paper, to tie them round with a string, and then to clip the paper close and neat all round, until it looked as smart as a pot of ointment from the apothecary's shop.[4] When a certain number of pots had attained this pitch of perfection, I was to paste on each a printed label, and then go on again with more pots. Two or three other boys were

[1] ***blacking:*** polish
[2] ***six shillings:*** 30p
[3] ***wainscoted:*** wood panelled
[4] ***apothecary's shop:*** chemist's shop

kept at similar duty downstairs on similar wages. One of them came up, in a ragged apron and a paper cap, on the first Monday morning, to show me the trick of using the string, and tying the knot. His name was Bob Fagin, and I took the liberty of using his name long afterwards in *Oliver Twist*.

Our relative had kindly arranged to teach me something in the dinner-hour, from twelve to one, I think it was, every day. But an arrangement so incompatible with counting-house business soon died away, from no fault of his or mine; and for the same reason my small work-table and my pots, my papers, string, scissors, paste pot and labels, by little and little, vanished out of the recess in the counting-house, and kept company with the other small work-tables, pots, papers, string, scissors and paste-pots downstairs. It was not long before Bob Fagin and I, and another boy whose name was Paul Green, worked generally side by side. Bob Fagin was an orphan and lived with his brother-in-law, a waterman.[5] Paul Green's father had the additional distinction of being a fireman.

No words can express the secret agony of my soul as I sunk into this companionship and felt my early hopes of growing up to be a learned and distinguished man crushed in my breast. The deep remembrance of the sense I had of being utterly neglected and hopeless – of the shame I felt in my position – of the misery it was to my young heart to believe that, day by day, what I had learned and thought and delighted in, and raised my fancy and my emulation up by, was passing away from me, never to be brought back any more – cannot be written. My whole nature was so penetrated with the grief and humiliation of such considerations that, even now, I wander desolately back to that time of my life.

---

[5] **waterman:** a skilled boatman

Margaret Thatcher in a Chocolate Factory

Frank Johnson

Frank Johnson was Parliamentary sketch-writer for the Daily Telegraph *and later* The Times. *Here, however, he writes about Conservative leader Margaret Thatcher when she was still Leader of the Opposition. One wonders what the factory workers made of the visit, which took place in 1979.*

Finding herself by chance in the extremely marginal constituency of Selly Oak – Labour majority 326 – she decided to call in on the voters on the Cadbury assembly line. It was a discreet visit – just the leader of the Opposition and about a hundred television and Press photographers and reporters.

Before we disgorged into the factory we all had to put on white coats and hats to make us hygienic. We then advanced on the unsuspecting folk on the conveyor belts. The famous factory is as superbly organised as legend has it, but is rather noisy. Apparently the manufacture of chocolate is a process which makes a noise like Niagara Falls. Into this existing uproar erupted Mrs Thatcher pursued by a hundred white coats. The whole effect resembled perhaps a lunatic asylum in which the doctors had themselves gone berserk;[1] or possibly a convention of mad surgeons.

Mrs Thatcher would descend on a chocolate woman (that is to say a woman making chocolate). They would have a conversation. Because of the din, neither could hear the other. This is the ideal arrangement for conversations between party leaders and voters at election time since it cuts out a lot of unnecessary detail.

Meanwhile, Mr Denis Thatcher the husband would lurk on the fringe of the affray conversing with employees who did not quite get to talk to his wife. He has developed an impressive line in Duke of Edinburgh factory visit chat. It goes something like: 'Do you export much? ... Really? Africa as well ... but surely it would melt?'

---

1 **berserk:** frenziedly violent

Back at base, the Leader of the Opposition would invariably be urged to try chocolate packing herself. The problem, of course, would have been to stop her. Maniacally, she would raid the hazel crispy clusters and shove them in passing boxes. At this, those of the deranged doctors who had cameras would ecstatically close in with their tripods, lights and in the case of the TV men those strange objects which look like small bazookas[2] and are to do with the sound. Some of them would clamber on chairs and machines to get a better angle. Thus clustered together at many different levels, they became not just mad surgeons but mad Martian surgeons as a result of their extra, deformed electronic eyes and cables coming out of their heads.

What a scene! The genius at Conservative Central Office who thought it up must get a knighthood.

In the middle of it all, the little chocolate woman who was the object of Mrs Thatcher's rapt attention would rather tend to get forgotten. Eventually we would all move further on down the conveyor belt or up to the next floor, the entire progress taking place before the disbelieving gaze of the Cadbury's employees on the conveyor belts. From department to department there was no abating[3] of the noise. Squeals! roaring machinery! and Denis still doing his stuff: 'Fascinating ... but how do you get the walnut exactly in the middle of the fudge?'

It was occasionally hazardous for those of us caught up in the heavy, swaying throng. Machines bubbled and clattered within inches. The Leader of the Conservative Party, borne irresistibly on by the deranged mob, was herself at times fortunate not to be converted into a large mass of delicious hazel crispy cluster.

Next week, with luck, a cement factory!

---

2 **bazookas:** portable rocket-launchers
3 **abating:** lessening

A Shoe Factory in Aleppo in the 1990s

William Dalrymple

On their long journey to Xanadu, William Dalrymple and his friend Laura passed through Syria, where their guide, Krikor, showed them round his brother's shoe factory. This extract shows how travel writing can contain elements of reportage.

Never have I seen a place like the Bekarion shoe factory. It lay at the bottom of a flight of stairs [so] we left our escort at ground level and descended into the hot, hammering depths. Krikor's brother sat like a Mogul[1] on a raised dais[2] at one end of the room, while all around him machines whirled and clattered. The floor was littered with old pieces of cut leather, and half-made or discarded shoes cluttered the bench tops. Around the debris buzzed a workforce of ragged children. Apart from Krikor's brother and a pock-marked foreman with a cadaverous grin,[3] none of the factory staff had yet reached puberty. I asked Krikor who the children were.

'Why aren't they at school?'

'Because my brother has bought them.'

'Bought them?'

'Yes. Their parents are poor and they want money for raki.[4] So they lease their children to my brother for one year.'

'And does your brother pay them?'

'Don't be stupid. If he paid them there would be no profit.'

'But that's slavery.' Krikor shrugged his shoulders.

'They like it here. My brother feeds them, and they enjoy themselves. Look, they are all happy.'

A little boy came up with two cups of Turkish coffee and a saucer full of salted melon seeds. He looked absolutely miserable.

---

[1] **Mogul:** Indian prince

[2] **dais:** platform

[3] **cadaverous grin:** ghastly grin like a corpse

[4] **raki:** strong alcoholic spirit, distilled from grain

'It's disgraceful,' said Laura.
'It's profit,' said Krikor.

Activities

Understanding
Match Girls

1 Briefly describe a typical day's work for a match girl. What might go wrong?
2 A match girl's salary of 4 shillings a week is described as 'splendid'. Is it really splendid? Explain why the author has used this word.
3 Explain in your own words why the match girls hated the statue of Gladstone.

Sixteen Ton

4 Approximately how far did Buddy travel each day to get to and from work?
5 How did the employers prevent their workers from earning actual money in the mines?

A Blacking Warehouse in the 1820s

6 List the five stages of Charles Dickens's work in the blacking factory.
7 What did Charles Dickens find most distressing about working in the blacking factory?

Margaret Thatcher in a Chocolate Factory

8 What was the purpose of Margaret Thatcher's visit to the chocolate factory?
9 The work being done in this extract is not its central concern, but how many different jobs are actually described? Make a list and compare it with a partner's.

A Shoe Factory in Aleppo in the 1990s

10 Why do the children work in the shoe factory for no wages?
11 What impression of the work being done in the shoe factory is given by the sentence 'Around the debris buzzed a workforce of ragged children'?

Style
Match Girls

12 The first part of this extract gives facts and figures, the latter part uses more emotional language to describe the match girls' plight. Pick out an example of each type of writing and say why you think it is effective.

13 Annie Besant compares the match girls to slaves at some length. What makes this comparison effective?

Sixteen Ton

14 This extract uses a very colloquial style. What are the advantages and disadvantages of using the 'voice' of an actual worker to describe his work and working conditions?

15 What devices does Studs Terkel use to give the impression that this piece is the record of someone speaking?

A Blacking Warehouse in the 1820s

16 Who is the intended audience of this autobiographical account? How can you tell?

17 Which parts of the description of the blacking factory let you know how Dickens felt about the place before you get to his explicit statement of feelings in the final paragraph?

Margaret Thatcher in a Chocolate Factory

18 How does Frank Johnson use comparisons to establish a humorous tone in this extract? Choose one or two and explain how they work.

19 Johnson makes several references to madness in this account. How do these contribute to its humour and what do they tell you about Frank Johnson's attitude towards Mrs Thatcher?

A Shoe Factory in Aleppo in the 1990s

20 The fact that the factory is staffed by children is not revealed until the end of the description. Why do you think William Dalrymple held this information back?

21 The extract ends with the lines:
    'It's disgraceful,' said Laura.
    'It's profit,' said Krikor.
What is the effect of placing these two statements with very similar formats but very different meanings side by side?

Speaking and listening

22 ◯ Work in groups of three or four. Each person picks a different extract and takes on the role of one of the workers described in it. As a group compare and contrast your working conditions.

Comparisons

23 'Match Girls', 'A Blacking Warehouse in the 1820s' and 'A Shoe Factory in Aleppo in the 1990s' all describe children working. What do we learn of the

◯ Speaking and listening work

attitudes to work of the children in each extract? Why are children more likely to be exploited at work than adults?

24 You could say that the coal miners' employees in 'Sixteen Ton' and the chocolate factory employees in 'Margaret Thatcher in a Chocolate Factory' are being exploited. In what ways are the two groups of workers being abused? Is either type of exploitation justifiable? Spend time researching exploitation in the workplace and hold a class debate.

Further activities

25 Design an advertisement for a local newspaper for any of the jobs in this section. Your ad must be truthful but it must also make the work sound attractive.

26 Choose one of the above extracts and then write a letter to a local newspaper, explaining why the factory described in it should be closed down.

Armed Conflict

If fighting breaks out today, the world can watch it on television only a few hours later. Information floods in bewilderingly fast. There is wall-to-wall reportage, 24 hours a day.

It was not always like that. Remember first of all that there has not been a successful invasion of Britain since 1066. This means that Britain's battles usually took place a long way from home; and news about the fighting came from two sources. First there were newspaper reports. These in turn received their information from official announcements which were by definition somewhat bald and lacking in the personal insights which make for good reportage. In 1798 the news of Nelson's victory in Abu Qir Bay was brought to the Admiralty by the fastest ship available; then an official communiqué was passed to *The Gazette* and *The Times*.

The second source of information was of course the people who were there and lived to tell the tale: people like John Nichols, Winston Churchill, Robert Graves. Their eyewitness accounts add precious detail and human interest to the official reports.

Kipling, on the other hand, was not a seaman, nor an engineer; he was a wordsmith struggling to come to terms with the might of even a modest Navy warship. No official statistics – size, tonnage, number and size of guns and so on – could convey its sheer, awesome power.

The Battle of the Nile

John Nichol

Everyone remembers Admiral Lord Nelson; but he owed his success to the skill and bravery of men like John Nichol, the narrator of this piece of reportage.

Imagine two fleets of mighty warships, each armed with up to a hundred cannon, firing iron balls weighing up to 15kg, smashing an enemy ship's sides or crippling her rigging. There were no engines: these ships relied on their huge canvas sails and on the courage and expertise of the men who sailed them.

There is one thing in Nichol's story from 1798 which you may find surprising: the presence of young boys and women on these fighting ships. In those days boys as young as nine or ten went to sea and did hard, dangerous duty. Also, it was possible for women to go to sea with their men if the captain allowed it.

The sun was just setting as we went into the bay, and a red and fiery sun it was. I would, if I had had my choice, have been on the deck; there I would have seen what was passing, and the time would not have hung so heavy; but every man does his duty with spirit, whether his station be in the slaughter-house or in the magazine.[1] (The seamen call the lower deck, near the main-mast, 'the slaughter-house', as it is amidships, and the enemy aim their fire principally at the body of the ship.) My station was in the powder-magazine with the gunner.

As we entered the bay we stripped to our trousers, opened our ports,[2] cleared, and every ship we passed gave them a broadside[3] and three cheers. Any information we got, was from the boys and women who carried the powder. They behaved as well as the men, and got a present for their bravery from the Grand Signior. When the French

---

[1] **magazine:** ammunition store
[2] **ports:** small openings in the side of a ship through which guns fire
[3] **gave them a broadside:** fired all the guns on one side of the ship at once

Admiral's ship blew up, the *Goliath* got such a shake we thought the after-part of her had blown up, until the boys told us what it was. They brought us every now and then the cheering news of another French ship having surrendered, and we answered the cheers on deck with heartfelt joy. In the heat of the action, a shot came right into the magazine, but did no harm, as the carpenters plugged it up, and stopped the water that was rushing in. I was much indebted to the gunner's wife, who gave her husband and me a drink of wine every now and then, which lessened our fatigue much. There were some of the women wounded, and one woman died of her wounds, and was buried on a small island in the bay. One woman bore a son in the heat of the action.

When we ceased firing, I went on deck to view the state of the fleets, and an awful sight it was. The whole bay was covered with dead bodies, mangled, wounded and scorched, not a bit of clothes on them except their trousers. There were a number of French belonging to the French Admiral's ship, the *L'Orient*, who had swum to the *Goliath*, and were cowering under her forecastle.[4] Poor fellows! they were brought on board, and Captain Foley ordered them down to the steward's room, to get provisions and clothing. They were thankful for our kindness, but were sullen and downcast as if each had lost a ship of his own.

The only incidents I heard of are two. One lad who was stationed by a salt-box, on which he sat to give out cartridges and keep the lid closed – it is a trying berth – when asked for a cartridge, he gave none, yet he sat upright; his eyes were open. One of the men gave him a push; he fell all his length on the deck. There was not a blemish on his body, yet he was quite dead, and was thrown overboard.

The other was a lad who had a match in his hand to fire his gun. In the act of applying it, a shot took off his arm; it hung by a small piece of skin. The match fell to the deck. He looked to his arm and, seeing

---

[4] **her forecastle:** the front section of the ship where the crew's quarters and storage areas are

what had happened, seized the match in his left hand, and fired off the gun before he went off to the cockpit[5] to have it dressed. They were in our mess,[6] or I might never have heard of it. Two of the mess were killed, and I knew not of it until the day after. Thus terminated the glorious first of August, the busiest night in my life.

[5] **the cockpit:** where the surgeon was
[6] **mess:** group of seamen who ate together

Target Practice

Rudyard Kipling

In 1897 Rudyard Kipling, who is better known for stirring poetry and collections of stories such as The Jungle Book *and* Plain Tales from the Hills, *was invited to go out on exercises with the Channel Fleet. By this time, engines had of course largely replaced sails; and shells and bullets had replaced cannonballs and canister.*

Descend by the slippery steel ladders into the bluish copper-smelling haze of hurrying mechanism all crowded under the protective deck; crawl along the greasy foot-plates, and stand with your back against the lengthwise bulkhead that separates the desperately whirling twin engines. Wait under the low-browed supporting-columns till the roar and the quiver has soaked into every nerve of you; till your knees loosen and your heart begins to pump. Try now to read the dizzying gauge-needles or find a meaning in the rumbled signals from the bridge. Creep into the stoke-hold – a boiler blistering either ear as you stoop – and taste what tinned air is like for a while.

No description will make you realise the almost infernal mobility of a Fleet at sea. I had seen cruisers flown like hawks, ridden like horses at a close finish, and manoeuvred like bicycles. Remember, we were merely a third-class cruiser, capable perhaps of slaying destroyers in a heavy sea, but meant for the most part to scout and observe. Our armament consisted of eight four-inch quick-fire wire guns, the newest type – two on the foc'sle,[1] four in the waist,[2] and two on the poop,[3] alternating with as many three-pounder Hotchkiss quick-firers.[4] Three Maxims[5]

---

[1] **foc'sle:** (forecastle) the front section of a ship where the crew's quarters and storage areas are

[2] **waist:** middle part of a ship

[3] **poop:** raised deck at the back of a ship

[4] **Hotchkiss quick-firers:** guns with revolving barrels (named after their inventor Benjamin Hotchkiss)

[5] **Maxims:** water-cooled machine guns (named after their inventor Hiram Maxim)

adorned the low nettings. Their water-jackets were filled up from an innocent tin-pot before the game began. It looked like slaking the thirst of devils.

We found an eligible rock, the tip of a greyish headland, peopled by a few gulls – the surge creaming along its base – and a portion of this we made our target, that we might see the effect of the shots and practise the men at firing on a water-line. Up came the beautiful solid brass cordite cartridges; and the four-inch shells that weigh twenty-five pounds apiece. The filled belts of the Maxims were adjusted, and all these man-slaying devices waked to life and peered over the side at the unsuspecting gulls. From the upper bridge I could hear, above the beat of the engines, the click of the lieutenants' scabbards (why should men who need every freedom in action be hampered by an utterly useless sword?). On his platform over my head the Navigating Officer was giving the range to the rock.

'Two thousand seven hundred yards, sir.'

'Two thousand seven hundred yards' – the order passed from gun to gun – 'ten knots right deflection – starboard battery.' The long lean muzzles shifted fractionally.

'Try a sighting shot with that three-pounder!'

There was the smell of cordite, then a shrillish gasping wail – exactly like the preliminary whoop of a hysterical woman – as the little shell hurried to its target; and a puff of dirty smoke on the rock-face sent the gulls flying. So far as I could observe there was not even a haze round the lips of the gun. Till I saw the spent case jerked out, I did not know which of the clean, precise, and devilish four had spoken.

'Two thousand four hundred,' the voice droned overhead, and the starboard bow four-inch quick-firer opened the ball. Again no smoke; again the song of the shell – not a shriek this time, but a most utterly mournful wail. Again the few seconds' suspense (what will they be when the Real Thing comes?) and a white star on the target. The cruiser winced a little as though someone had pinched her.

Before the next gun had fired, the empty cartridge cylinder of the first was extracted, and by some sleight of hand I could not see the breech had closed behind a full charge.

'Two thousand three hundred,' cried the reader of that day's lessons, and we fell seriously to work; high shriek and low wail following in an infernal fugue,[6] through which, with no regard for decency, the Maxims quacked and jabbered insanely. The rock was splintered and ripped and gashed in every direction, and great pieces of it bounded into the sea.

'Two thousand one hundred.'

'Good shot. Oh, good shot! ... Ah – ah! Bad. Damn bad! Short! Miles short! Who fired that shot?'

A shell had burst short of the mark, and the captain of that gun was asked politely if he supposed Government supplied him with three-pound shell for the purpose of shooting mackerel.

And so we went on, till the big guns had fired their quota and the Maxims ran out in one last fiends' flurry, and target-practice for the month was over. The rock that had been grey was white, and a few shining cartridge-cases lay beside each gun.

Then the horror of the thing began to soak into me. What I had seen was a slow peddling-out of the Admiralty allowance for the month, and it seemed to me more like squirting death through a hose than any ordinary gun-practice. What will it be when all the ammunition-hoists are working, when the Maxims' water-jacket puffs off in steam; when the three-pounder charges come up a dozen at a time to be spent twenty to the minute; when the sole limit of four-inch fire is the speed with which the shells and cases can be handled?

What will it be when the Real Thing is upon us?

---

[6] **fugue:** complicated, repeated musical composition

The North-West Frontier

Winston Churchill

In the 1890s Winston (later Sir Winston) Churchill served as an army officer in India and on the North-West Frontier. Here is his account (published in 1941) of the first time he saw action.

I lay down with an officer and eight Sikhs on the side of the village towards the mountain, whilst the remainder of the company rummaged about the mud houses or sat down and rested behind them. A quarter of an hour passed and nothing happened. Then the captain of the company arrived.

'We are going to withdraw,' he said to the subaltern.[1] 'You stay here and cover our retirement till we take up a fresh position on that knoll below the village.' He added, 'The Buffs[2] don't seem to be coming up, and the colonel thinks we are rather in the air here.'

It struck me that this was a sound observation. We waited another ten minutes. Meanwhile I presumed, for I could not see them, the main body of the company was retiring from the village towards the lower knoll. Suddenly the mountainside sprang to life. Swords flashed from behind rocks, bright flags waved here and there. A dozen widely-scattered white smoke-puffs broke from the rugged face in front of us. Loud explosions resounded close at hand. From high up on the crag, one thousand, two thousand, three thousand feet above us, white or blue figures appeared, dropping down the mountainside from ledge to ledge like monkeys down the branches of a tall tree. A shrill crying arose from many points. Yi! Yi! Yi! Bang! Bang! Bang! The whole hillside began to be spotted with smoke, and tiny figures descended every moment nearer towards us. Our eight Sikhs opened an independent fire, which soon became more and more rapid. The hostile figures continued to flow down the mountainside, and scores began to gather in rocks

---

[1] **subaltern:** junior officer
[2] **The Buffs:** East Kent Regiment

about a hundred yards away from us. The targets were too tempting to be resisted. I borrowed the Martini[3] of the Sikh by whom I lay. He was quite content to hand me cartridges. I began to shoot carefully at the men gathering in the rocks. A lot of bullets whistled about us. But we lay very flat, and no harm was done. This lasted perhaps five minutes in continuous crescendo. We had certainly found the adventure for which we had been looking. Then an English voice close behind. It was the battalion adjutant.

'Come on back now. There is no time to lose. We can cover you from the knoll.'

The Sikh whose rifle I had borrowed had put eight or ten cartridges on the ground beside me. It was a standing rule to let no ammunition fall into the hands of the tribesmen. The Sikh seemed rather excited, so I handed him the cartridges one after the other to put in his pouch. This was a lucky inspiration. The rest of our party got up and turned to retreat. There was a ragged volley from the rocks; shouts, exclamations and a scream. I thought for the moment that five or six of our men had lain down again. So they had: two killed and three wounded. One man was shot through the breast and was pouring with blood; another lay on his back kicking and twisting. The British officer was spinning round just behind me, his face a mass of blood, his right eye cut out. Yes, it was certainly an adventure.

It is a point of honour on the Indian frontier not to leave wounded men behind. Death by inches and hideous mutilation are the invariable measure meted out to all who fall in battle into the hands of the Pathan tribesmen. Back came the adjutant,[4] with another British officer of subaltern rank, a Sikh sergeant-major, and two or three soldiers. We all laid hands on the wounded and began to carry and drag them away down the hill. We got through the few houses, ten or twelve men carrying four, and emerged upon a bare strip of ground. Here stood the captain commanding the company with half-a-dozen men. Beyond and

---

[3] **Martini:** rifle
[4] **adjutant:** assistant to a superior officer

below, one hundred and fifty yards away, was the knoll on which a supporting party should have been posted. No sign of them! Perhaps it was the knoll lower down. We hustled the wounded along, regardless of their protests. We had no rearguard[5] of any kind. All were carrying the wounded. I was therefore sure that worse was close at our heels. We were not half-way across the open space when twenty or thirty furious figures appeared among the houses, firing frantically and waving their swords.

I could only follow by fragments what happened after that. One of the two Sikhs helping to carry my wounded man was shot through the calf. He shouted with pain; his turban fell off; and his long black hair streamed over his shoulders. Two more men came from below and seized hold of our man. The new subaltern and I got the [wounded man] by the collar and dragged him along the ground. Luckily it was all down hill. Apparently we hurt him so much on the sharp rocks that he asked to be let go alone. He hopped and crawled and staggered and stumbled, but made a good pace. Thus he escaped.

I looked round to my left. The adjutant had been shot. Four of his soldiers were carrying him. He was a heavy man, and they all clutched at him. Out from the edge of the houses rushed half a dozen Pathan swordsmen. The bearers of the poor adjutant let him fall and fled at their approach. The leading tribesman rushed upon the prostrate figure and slashed at it three or four times with his sword.

I forgot everything at this moment except a desire to kill this man. I wore my long cavalry sword well sharpened. After all, I had won the public schools fencing medal. I resolved on personal combat. The savage saw me coming. I was not more than twenty yards away. He picked up a big stone and hurled it at me with his left hand, and then awaited me, brandishing his sword.

There were others waiting not far behind him. I changed my mind about the cold steel. I pulled out my revolver, took, as I thought, most careful aim, and fired. No result. I fired again. No result. I fired again.

---

[5] **rearguard:** soldiers who protect the rear of a military formation

Whether I hit him or not I cannot tell. At any rate he ran back two or three yards and plumped down behind a rock. The fusillade[6] was continuous. I looked around. I was all alone with the enemy. Not a friend was to be seen. I ran as fast as I could. There were bullets everywhere. I got to the first knoll. Hurrah, there were the Sikhs holding the lower one! They made vehement gestures, and in a few moments I was among them.

There was still about three quarters of a mile of the spur to traverse before the plain was reached, and on each side of us other spurs ran downwards. Along these rushed our pursuers, striving to cut us off and firing into both our flanks. I don't know how long we took to get to the bottom. But it was all done quite slowly and steadfastly. We carried two wounded officers and about six wounded Sikhs with us. That took about twenty men. We left one officer and a dozen men dead and wounded to be cut to pieces on the spur.

During this business I armed myself with the Martini and ammunition of a dead man, and fired as carefully as possible thirty or forty shots at tribesmen on the left-hand ridge at distances from eighty to a hundred and twenty yards. The difficulty about these occasions is that one is so out of breath and quivering with exertion, if not with excitement. However, I am sure I never fired without taking aim. We fetched up at the bottom of the spur little better than a mob, but still with our wounded. There was the company reserve and the lieutenant-colonel commanding the battalion and a few orderlies. [The tribesmen were kept at bay until the Buffs arrived.]

---

[6] **fusillade:** rapid fire

In the Trenches

Robert Graves

Robert Graves is perhaps best known for I Claudius, *which was made into a successful television series; but in* Goodbye to All That *(1929) he describes his experiences as an officer in the First World War.*

The next two days we spent in bivouacs[1] outside Mametz wood. We were in fighting kit and felt cold at night, so I went into the wood to find German overcoats to use as blankets. It was full of dead Prussian Guards Reserve, big men, and dead Royal Welch and South Wales Borderers of the New Army battalions, little men. Not a single tree in the wood remained unbroken. I collected my overcoats, and came away as quickly as I could, climbing through the wreckage of green branches. Going and coming, by the only possible route, I passed by the bloated and stinking corpse of a German with his back propped against a tree. He had a green face, spectacles, close-shaven hair; black blood was dripping from his nose and beard. I came across two other unforgettable corpses: a man of the South Wales Borderers and one of the Lehr Regiment had succeeded in bayoneting each other simultaneously. A survivor of the fighting told me later that he had seen a young soldier of the Fourteenth Royal Welch bayoneting a German in parade-ground style, automatically exclaiming: 'In, out, on guard!'

I was still superstitious about looting or collecting souvenirs. 'These greatcoats are only a loan,' I told myself. Our brigade, the Nineteenth, was the reserve brigade; the other brigades, the Ninety-ninth and Hundredth, had attacked Martinpuich two days previously, but been halted with heavy losses as soon as they started. We were left to sit about in shell-holes and watch our massed artillery blazing away, almost wheel to wheel. On the 18th, we advanced to a position just north of Bazentin-le-Petit, and relieved the Tyneside Irish. I had been posted to 'D' Company. Our Irish guide was hysterical and had

---

[1] **bivouacs:** temporary encampments

forgotten the way; we put him under arrest and found it ourselves. On the way up through the ruins of Bazentin-le-Petit, we were shelled with regard to gas-shells. The standing order with gas-shells was not to bother about respirators, but push on. Hitherto, they had all been lachrymatory ones;[2] these were the first of the deadly kind, so we lost half a dozen men.

When at last 'D' Company reached the trenches, scooped beside a road and not more than three feet deep, the badly shaken Tyneside company we were relieving hurried off, without any of the usual formalities. I asked their officers where the Germans were. He said he didn't know, but pointed vaguely towards Martinpuich, a mile to our front. Then I asked him who held our left flank, and how far off they were. He didn't know. I damned his soul to Hell as he went away. Having got into touch with 'C' Company behind us on the right, and the Fourth Suffolks fifty yards to the left, we began deepening the trenches and presently located the Germans – in a trench system some five hundred yards to our front, keeping fairly quiet.

The next day, at dinnertime, very heavy shelling started: shells bracketed along the trench about five yards short and five yards over, but never quite got it. Three times running, my cup of tea was spilled by the concussion and filled with dirt. I happened to be in a cheerful mood, and just laughed ... A tame magpie had come into the trench; apparently belonging to the Germans driven out of the village by the Gordon Highlanders a day or two before. It looked very bedraggled. 'That's one for sorrow,' I said. The men swore that it made some remark in German as it joined us, and talked of wringing its neck.

Being now off duty, I fell asleep in the trench without waiting for the bombardment to stop. It would be no worse getting killed asleep than awake. There were no dug-outs, of course. I found it quite easy to sleep through bombardments; though vaguely conscious of the noise, I let it go by. Yet if anyone came to wake me for my watch, or shouted 'Stand-to!', I was always alert in a second. I could fall asleep sitting down,

---

[2] **lachrymatory ones:** tear gas shells

standing, marching, lying on a stone floor or in any other position, at a moment's notice at any time of the day or night. But on this occasion I had a fearful nightmare of somebody handling me secretly, choosing a place to drive a knife into me. Finally, he gripped me in the small of the back. I woke up with a start, shouting, punched at the assassin's hand – and found I had killed a mouse which had run down my neck for fear of the shells.

Activities

Understanding
The Battle of the Nile

1 Briefly retell these events from the point of view of a French sailor on *L'Orient*.

2 What impression of the characters of ordinary English sailors does this extract suggest? Give reasons for your answer.

Target Practice

3 How does Rudyard Kipling try to give a sense of the mobility of the fleet in the second paragraph?

4 State in your own words what Kipling means by the 'Real Thing'. Why do you think he refers to it twice in the extract?

The North-West Frontier

5 Explain why it was decided that Churchill's unit should withdraw from the village.

6 Reread the extract carefully and draw a labelled diagram of Churchill's retreat.

In the Trenches

7 What causes Robert Graves most trouble in this extract? His own side or the enemy? Give reasons for your answer.

8 How much time passes in this extract, and how much fighting does Graves engage in?

9 Which of the following would make a good subheading for this extract?
   • 'The horror of war'
   • 'The boredom of war'
   • 'The reality of war'.
   Give reasons for your choice.

Style
The Battle of the Nile

10 Find examples of colloquial style used in this extract. Do you think it was written by the gunner himself or do you think it was retold to someone else? Give reasons for your answer.

11 Look at the sentence that begins 'As we entered the bay ... '. What impression does running the many stages of the battle together in this manner give?

Target Practice

12 The first paragraph of this extract reads as a series of instructions:
'Descend ... ', 'Wait ... ' and so on. How does this technique help you to
imagine the conditions on board ship?

13 Kipling often uses the brand names of guns such as Martini, Maxim and
Hotchkiss, and assumes that his audience will be also be familiar with them.
How does this affect our attitude to the guns?

14 Throughout the extract Kipling makes references to hell and devils. How do
these comparisons affect our attitude to the events described?

The North-West Frontier

15 Churchill twice states that this episode is an adventure. Find the two
statements and describe how they differ in their impact.

16 Churchill tells us what he did but seldom mentions how he feels. Do you
think the passage would have been better if Churchill had mentioned his
feelings? Or would they have got in the way of the action? Give reasons for
your answer.

In the Trenches

17 Robert Graves gives a great deal of detail about the different military units
engaged in the battle. This is likely to be confusing to an outsider so why do
you think he included it?

18 Why do you think Graves has included the details of the magpie and the
mouse in his description of a war zone?

Speaking and listening

19 ⬭ In pairs or small groups, discuss whether you would fight in a war or
not. Talk as fully as possible about why you might or might not fight and
then report your discussion to the rest of the class.

20 ⬭ Imagine you fought in a war a long time ago. What would you tell your
grandchildren? Either act out such a conversation with a partner or discuss
what kind of things you might say. Would you try to make war seem like an
adventure or an horrific ordeal?

Comparisons

21 In all of the extracts involving death, some deaths are described in detail and
some are stated matter-of-factly. What do the detailed descriptions of death
seem to have in common?

22 Compare Robert Graves's and Winston Churchill's accounts of warfare.
Which gives you the best impression of what it might be like to fight in a
war? Why?

⬭ Speaking and listening work

23 All of these extracts are written in the first person. Give as many reasons as you can for why the authors have chosen this method.

Further activities

24 Write an eyewitness account of an exciting event you have taken part in. You might try to convey a sense of the excitement or you could deal with the mundane reality of your event: the crowds, the trouble you had parking, your anxiety at missing something and so on.

25  Discuss with your class why people seem to find death and violence such fascinating topics.

 Speaking and listening work

Playtime

'Playtime' deals with just a few of the things people get up to in their free time: paintballing – 'War Games', sport – 'Duel of the Four-Minute Milers', 'What's My Name?' and 'United Seize Glory in Photo Finish', and watching television – 'Get Some Real Actors!'

Sports commentators add the flesh to the bare bones of the results. Which would you rather read? 'Manchester United 2, Bayern Munich 1', or a piece of reportage like 'United Seize Glory in Photo Finish'?

Television critics breathe on our own poor, inadequate, half-articulated opinions and make of them something incisive and eloquent. How often have *you* glared at *EastEnders* and muttered, 'Why don't they get some *real* actors?' Caitlin Moran manages to say the same thing, far more elegantly, in *The Times*.

What's My Name?

Alistair Cooke

In February 1967 Muhammad Ali, formerly known as Cassius Clay, became the undisputed heavyweight champion of the world after having been deprived of his title on a technicality. Later that year he was sentenced to prison, and again stripped of his title, after refusing military service on religious grounds. He had his title restored in 1970, and lost and regained it twice (which is unique in boxing history) before retiring in 1981.

In Houston, Texas, last night, Muhammad Ali of Louisville, Kentucky, became the first Black Muslim priest to be acclaimed as the undisputed heavyweight champion of the world. His comment was in keeping with his holy calling, 'I am a miracle.'

Until the final bell clanged, after fifteen rounds of teasing slaughter, Ernie Terrell, a modest giant from Philadelphia, was the official World Boxing Association champion, on the technicality that he had dutifully fought the opponents sanctioned by the association, whereas Muhammad Ali was disbarred as a reputable fighter when Sonny Liston retired hurt and he promptly signed him up for a lucrative return bout.

But shortly before midnight, when Terrell looked like a broken-down sledgehammer being pawed by a tiger, there was no doubt in anyone's mind, least of all in Terrell's, that his day was done. He has never been knocked down, and it was something of a collateral miracle that his 6 foot 6 inch frame could still potter around with a left eye as plump as a June strawberry and his right like a bloody slit left by the Vietcong. This mountain had come to Muhammad and had been blasted apart in one hour and ten minutes of calculated detonations.

According to his conqueror, it was all his own fault. Muhammad had said earlier in the day that at the weighing-in he would ask Terrell a simple question of three words, and according to the answer he would either dispose of him in a merciful knockout or stretch him out on the rack of a long, humiliating defeat.

The question was: 'What's my name?' The answer, respected by all sports writers and fight fans, is Cassius Marcellus Clay, a very proud name in Kentucky since it is that of the delegate who secured the presidential nomination of Abraham Lincoln, the man who, in a rare act of pre-vision, freed the slaves and enabled the present Cassius Clay to hate the white man and tool round in a Lincoln Continental.

But young Cassius recently brushed off the eminence[1] his parents hoped would brush off on him from his famous namesake. He took his Black Muslim vows, renounced tobacco, liquor and the wiles of women, and declared himself to be the one and only Muhammad Ali. At the weighing-in, Terrell stared at him as long as Scrooge recognising Marley's ghost and replied, 'I know him – Cassius Clay!' Clay went into his well-known dance of rage and promised Terrell slow torture from what appeared at the time to be motives of sheer meanness but which was later explained as an act of obedience to religious scruples.

Muhammad was as good as his sacred word. It took him six rounds to manoeuvre the infidel into the proper position for a ritual sacrifice. Like the roisterers[2] in the old Sunday School lantern slides, Terrell had the unbeliever's usual early luck. He kept planting Muhammad against the ropes and jabbing at his ribs, not only with the left that everyone credits him with but with right-arm stabs as well. But in the seventh round the rake's progress took its inevitable downhill turn. The man of God was out in the centre now, hopping and feinting[3] and tossing his head back in rhythm with the wild lunges of the 'one-armed bandit'.

The simple sinner could never reach him and pretty soon the slides would show us the falling-down drunk, the mortgage foreclosed, the weeping family and the triumph of virtue. There was blood on both of them by now but it came from the spouting eyelids of Terrell.

---

[1] **eminence:** distinction

[2] **roisterers:** merry-makers

[3] **feinting:** making movements to trick the opponent

In the eighth and ninth rounds Muhammad allowed him a pause for repentance. Jabbing and hooking and belting as he chose, Muhammad started to scream his catechism: 'What's my name? What's my name?' Terrell was too dumb, or beaten, to respond. For the last six interminable rounds, his head was hidden behind his gloves and from time to time he would peep through a veil of blood and give little left jabs, like an expiring cat.

Muhammad was greatly troubled by one snag in the plot. 'I had meant to put him away in the eighth,' he said, 'but he wouldn't go down'. By some foul-up of the moral order, Terrell suffered and survived his promised purgatory.

And the next fight? There would be no next fight, said Mohammad's manager or acolyte,[4] until they had gone with other good Muslims to Arabia. Next stop, Mecca (by permission of Muhammad's draft board, which blasphemously denies his divinity and has classified him 1-A: fit for potato peeling or Vietnam).

---

[4] **acolyte:** priest's assistant

War Games

Grace Bradberry

In the summer of 2000 Times *reporter Grace Bradberry took part in paintball war games in California.*

There are some safety warnings so disturbing that any good they might do is outweighed by the alarm, even panic, they engender. Certainly, when gathering for a spot of Saturday morning recreation, one doesn't want to hear the following broadcast over a loudspeaker: 'No real guns are to be used! Repeat – anyone found carrying a real gun will be asked to leave!' Welcome to paintballing in the American West, where a man might easily skip the cost of equipment hire and instead improvise with his own 'weapon'.

Paintballing in England may be a lark, the stuff of office outings and stag weekends. In California, it's a more serious proposition ... Improbable as it seems, paintballing is a hot activity among junior Hollywood executives and from time to time up to a hundred of them will gather, summoned by e-mail for a day of battle where one set of executives battles another ...

The Hollywood tribe were not difficult to spot when they did arrive, piling out of a series of black cars and Sports Utility Vehicles, in Abercrombie and Fitch pants and wraparound sunglasses ... They might be fearless in the face of an aggressive business adversary, but these Beverley Hills ninjas[1] were as nervous as I was at the sight of the hordes of militaristic locals. As we watched an induction video, there was anxious laughter as it reiterated the warning about real guns. But by the time we'd hired camouflage clothing and helmets, we more or less blended into the surroundings.

Nothing, however, prepared me for 'war zones'. Paintballing in England might involve haring through the Forest of Dean. But in Riverside County there were mock-ups of every major war in which

---

[1] **ninjas:** Japanese fighters

Americans have died since the Forties. Vietnam, in which we fought our first war, was all undergrowth and foliage. Despite the good cover, I was hit on the head within the first ten seconds. We moved on to Beirut – shelled-out buildings and little cover – then North Korea, which was a bit like Vietnam but less leafy. But we passed on Germany 1945, and the Gulf War. Perhaps the owners are planning to add Sierra Leone. I didn't like to ask.

Duel of the Four-Minute Milers

Paul O'Neil

In May 1954 Englishman Dr Roger Bannister ran the first four-minute mile. Six weeks later Australia's John Landy ran the second. That August, in the Empire Games, both men broke the four-minute barrier in the same race.

At first glance they seemed like an odd pair of gladiators. Like most distance men both look frail and thin in street clothes. Landy has a mop of dark, curly hair, the startled brown eyes of a deer, a soft voice with little trace of the Australian snarl, and a curious habit of bending forward and clasping his hands before his chest when making a controversial point ... [Bannister] too would be the last man in the world to be singled out of a crowd as an athlete. He is stooped and negligent in carriage; he has lank blond hair, a high-cheeked, peaked face and a polite and non-committal upper-class British voice ...

They ran Landy first, Bannister second at the end of the stretch and the duel had begun. 'Time for the first lap,' the loudspeakers grated as they entered the turn, 'fifty-eight seconds.' Then bedlam[1] began too. It increased as Landy moved away – five yards, ten yards, fifteen yards – in the backstretch of the second lap, and Bannister let him go. 'It was a frightening thing to do,' said Bannister later, 'but I believed he was running too fast. I had to save for my final burst and hope I could catch him in time.'

Landy's time was 1:58 at the half. The groundwork for a four-minute mile had been laid. The field had faded far to the rear. The duellists ran alone in front with Landy still making the pace. But now, yard by yard, easily, almost imperceptibly Bannister was regaining ground. He was within striking distance as they fled into the last, decisive quarter amid a hysterical uproar of applause. He stayed there on the turn. Two hundred yards from home, Landy made his bid for decision and victory. But

---

[1] **bedlam:** a state of uproar

Bannister refused to be shaken, and with 90 yards to go he lengthened his plunging stride. He came up shoulder to shoulder, fought for momentum, pulled away to a four-yard lead and ran steadily and stylishly through a deafening clamour to the tape. He fell, arms flapping, legs buckling, into the arms of the English team manager a split second after the race.

Get Some Real Actors!

Caitlin Moran

Caitlin Moran had her first piece printed in The Times *when she was about the age of most* Cascades *readers. This piece appeared in October 2000.*

They've got one thing right – everyone *is* talking about *EastEnders*. They're wondering how, in a time when a thousand professional actors a day starve to death for the want of work as an armed blagger in a *Crimewatch* reconstruction, the entire Slater family appear to have been cast from a women's open-prison drama project. I mean, there's no way they can be real actors. In one or two cases, it's questionable whether they're even alive. There's certainly good reason to suspect Mo Slater is dead: her face is so impassive it's as if all her features were laid out on a tablecloth and not wired up at all; and when she shouts, she often. Stops in the middle, as if the golem[1]-spell in her head had temporarily run down.

Still, big-up to the casting director on one score: her screen granddaughters certainly give the impression it's hereditary. The absurdly slutty Kat bolts her lines like a navvy with a pastie, and the sulky dutiful one who runs the Caff flatly intones 'Leave it out' like a child learning the words from its words-tin, despite having the whole history of actors from *EastEnders* shouting 'Leave it out' to crib from.

Scenes involving the Slater family *en masse* exist in a curious hinterland where emotion is something unobtainable: it's like watching a row of concrete bollards trying to look concerned, a drawer full of string trying to run through the surf in *Chariots of Fire*. I rather suspect that somewhere along the line a terrible accident has occurred at the BBC: the Bhopal[2] of casting disasters. The cast of a new docusoap –

---

[1] **golem:** an artificially created human being, brought alive by supernatural means (in Jewish legend)

[2] **Bhopal:** Indian town in which an accident at a chemical works killed many people and left many more terminally sick

possibly *If I Act I'll Puff Up and Die* – were herded into the wrong room and mistakenly cast as the new family in *EastEnders*. Loath to give up a future that includes two No 17 singles and the possibility of a major drinking problem, the girls have kept *schtumm*;[3] while somewhere in another part of Britain, a camera crew are trailing around a bunch of luvvies going to auditions for the new Toilet Duck advert and wondering why their subjects aren't starting to swell up a bit.

Two weeks ago, the Slaters took a black cab down to Mo's daughter and the girls' mother's grave. Actors usually have so much fun standing around a grave. All in black in a neatly ordered field of death – wrestling with those memories, being brave, doing some anger, and then into a series of deep, hacking sobs while you try to hide your face with your hands. The Slaters just stood there like pressganged seven-year-olds playing the Three Wise Men, trying to remember in which order to show their gold, frankincense and myrrh.

Still, you can understand why the producers of *EastEnders* decided to do something as drastic as bring in soap's first family of radio-controlled corpses. *'stEnders* is going through a rough patch that's lasted nearly two years – obviously not as troubling as *Brookside*'s decade-long free-fall, but still worrying when anyone with UK Gold can travel back to the time of the Sharongate tapes twice a week. The *EastEnders* message board contains many sad little voices confirming this – most ably represented by 'Sapphire', who admits *'EastEnders* is getting kinda borin. im finding myself enjoying doin my homework betta lately.' [*sic*]

However, this has been a freakishly good week for *EastEnders*: Sonia popped to the bathroom for a bit of 'quiet time' and unexpectedly gave birth to a full-term baby – the kind of absurd television genius that, in ten years' time, nostalgists in their cups will get weepy over.

But it's going to take more than a poo that turned into Martin Fowler's baby to make *'stEnders* a proper treat again. Rather like a jellyfish trying to push a chest of drawers up some stairs, they just haven't got the structure to make this objective possible.

---

[3] **schtumm:** quiet

Soaps are formulaic: you need a king and a queen, a pretty princess, star-crossed lovers, a villain, a hero, a chorus and a buffoon. Instead, *EastEnders* 2000 has an amorphous mass of dullards (Terry, Beppe, Roy, Laura, the pointless Mel) drifting aimlessly through their lives, sporadically being asked by Pauline if they've seen Mark around.

Although it might sound stupid to try and marry the concept to a load of whining adulterous Cockerney veg-peddlers, there is no sense of a *greater destiny*. The only character with a bit of zip was Janine, who was shaping up to be the Alexis Colby[4] of Albert Square until they exiled her to the Caff, where she now puts horrible pink extensions in her hair, in much the same way as bored chimpanzees smear their poo on the walls in the zoo.

Which brings us back to the Slaters again.

---

[4] **Alexis Colby:** catty and powerful female character in the 1980s television series *Dynasty*

United Seize Glory in Photo Finish

Oliver Holt

Footballers are the new gladiators: heroes who perform wonders of skill and daring for the entertainment of the less heroic. The Roman writer Suetonius describes the fans who packed the Colosseum amphitheatre in Rome; each faction had its own colour; each had its own chants and its own ways of cheering on its favourite charioteers or gladiators. Suetonius does not say whether the fans went home after the games to drink from commemorative pottery or to sleep under bed covers printed with pictures of their heroes, but the resemblance is there.

May 26 1999 was a great day for the thousands of small and not-so-small boys who drink from Manchester United mugs and sleep under Manchester United duvet covers. Their heroes defeated Bayern Munich in Barceloma to add the European Cup to their FA Cup and Premiership title.

United last won the European Cup in 1968, in the glory days of George Best, Bobby Charlton and the late Sir Matt Busby. When the lads pulled it off again in 1999 – on Sir Matt's birthday – they were cheered on by a television audience of 500 million worldwide. That's a lot of Man. United mugs.

A thousand flashbulbs recorded the moment. When the final whistle went last night, they lit up the Nou Camp here as though it was noonday in the Barcelona sun and froze the Manchester United players with their arms in the air. It was the instant they passed into legend.

In two astonishing, almost surreal, minutes at the end of the last European Cup final of the twentieth century, the gilded youth of the most famous of clubs left excellence behind them and found the greatness they have been searching for.

The treble is theirs now, as well, something unprecedented, something that even the great English sides of the past have always fallen short of. It is unlikely that it will ever be repeated.

By coming from behind to beat Bayern Munich with two goals in the final minutes, by transforming what seemed like certain defeat into glorious, glorious victory, this United side escaped once and for all from the shadow of Sir Matt Busby and the team that won the trophy in 1968.

The problem for future United teams, for future teams of all nations for that matter, will not be in trying to recreate the magic of George Best and Bobby Charlton, it will be in the impossible task of trying to surpass the unsurpassable, of bettering a finish that could not be imagined.

The game had already entered its final minute of normal time when the comeback began. It had seemed that United had fallen to a tame defeat courtesy of a sixth-minute free kick from Mario Basler. They have developed a reputation for conjuring comebacks in Europe this season, but this time, against the resilience of the Germans, the match seemed to be out of reach.

Instead, Teddy Sheringham, who had been ridiculed this season for being a loser, scored in the ninetieth minute, just as he had scored in the FA Cup Final last Saturday. As Bayern were trying to adjust to that, Sheringham nodded on a Beckham corner and Ole Gunnar Solskjaer, who had only been on the pitch for eight minutes, hooked it into the roof of the net.

A few seconds later, the final whistle went and the Germans threw themselves to the floor as if they had the falling sickness. Carsten Jancker, who had hit the bar for Bayern ten minutes from the end, sobbed uncontrollably. Most of his team-mates looked stunned.

United were, of course, the souls of jubilation and wild celebration. As they stood in front of their supporters, Sheringham mimicked the action of sweeping in his equaliser and Dwight Yorke and Andy Cole danced a samba of delight in the centre circle. If there was any poignancy among the English, it was sympathy for Roy Keane and Paul Scholes, the men who had missed out because of suspension.

Yet the triumph was perhaps sweetest for Alex Ferguson, the United manager. He has suffered in Busby's shadow more than most, but now he can retire in three years knowing he has found the fulfilment that he deserves. It was he who took the gamble of playing Beckham in central midfield, he who risked everything by throwing on Sheringham and Solskjaer. It was his triumph more than anyone's and he admitted afterwards that he could hardly take it in.

'You cannot deny the most important fact of all,' Ferguson said, 'and that is the spirit and the will to win that exists at this club. That is what won the trophy for us tonight.

'It is the greatest night of my life. I was prepared to risk and if you risk in a game of football you deserve to succeed. Sheringham and Solskjaer are goalscorers and they are good at their job. They are terrific substitutes.

'I am proud of my heritage tonight. I am proud of my family. I was starting to adjust to defeat near the end, I kept saying to myself: "Keep your dignity and accept it is not your year."

'It is a fairytale. It would have been Sir Matt Busby's birthday today and I think he was doing a lot of kicking up there in the last couple of minutes. I suppose you could say we have come out of his shadow now, but, with all the team has achieved this year, they could not have had any question marks against them.

'This team plays the right way. They embrace every concept of football that I like. What they have achieved is unprecedented. Nobody has ever done it. They deserve it.'

When Ferguson had finished, he got up to leave. The room erupted in applause and the flashbulbs started flashing again.

Activities

Understanding
What's My Name?

1 State briefly the arguments for and against Muhammad Ali changing his name.

2 Do you think Muhammad Ali deliberately treated Terrell cruelly in the fight or was he simply not able to beat him as quickly as he had hoped? Give reasons for your answer.

War Games

3 What are the main differences between English paintballing and the American version of the activity?

4 Describe how you think the 'Beverley Hills ninjas' and 'militaristic locals' would have been dressed before they hired their camouflage gear.

Duel of the Four-Minute Milers

5 Describe the similarities and differences between Landy and Bannister.

6 Rewrite the description of the race as if it were an actual live commentary.

Get Some Real Actors!

7 Find at least two strengths and two weaknesses in the *EastEnders* episodes under discussion.

8 What, in Caitlin Moran's opinion, is the main problem with the soap opera?

United Seize Glory in Photo Finish

9 When did Manchester United first win the European Cup?

10 Name two Manchester United players from the two different teams that won the cup.

11 List all the goals scored in this match with times and scorers.

Style
What's My Name?

12 Alistair Cooke uses some striking comparisons in this extract. Choose two and describe why you find them effective.

13 Throughout the passage Cooke gives the fight religious significance. Find examples of the way he does this. How do you think these comments affect our opinion of Muhammad Ali?

War Games

14 There is an uneasy mixture of reality and fantasy in this article. What are the fantasy elements, and what are the disturbing elements of reality that Grace Bradberry focuses on?

15 Most of this article consists of long flowing sentences, but it finishes on a very short one. What is the effect of this on the reader?

Duel of the Four-Minute Milers

16 Look again at the descriptions of the two men. These could be described as 'thumbnail' sketches designed to give a quick impression of the athletes. List the qualities Paul O'Neil has picked out and then suggest other pieces of information, such as eye colour, that would help to give you a clearer picture of Landy and Bannister.

17 Look closely at the lengths of the sentences in the description of the race. How do they change? Why do you think O'Neil has constructed his sentences in this manner?

Get Some Real Actors!

18 What is unusual about the last two sentences of the first paragraph? Why has Caitlin Moran written them in this manner?

19 This article uses a number of slang terms but also talks of the soap opera's need for a sense of a 'greater destiny'. What is the effect of this mixture of seriousness and slang? What other techniques are used to create a similar effect?

United Seize Glory in Photo Finish

20 This report of a football match starts at the end. Explain as fully as you can why you think Oliver Holt has chosen to begin his account at this point.

21 How much background information is required to understand this article? Imagine you were about to republish it in a book for 2100. What words and names would you need to include notes on?

Speaking and listening

22 ⬭ With a partner, improvise a conversation between a person described in one of these articles and the journalist who wrote it. As the subject of the article, did you feel fairly treated by the journalist? As the journalist did you feel you had been fair in your criticism?

Comparisons

23 'Get Some Real Actors!' and 'United Seize Glory in Photo Finish' are both written for audiences who know a great deal about the subject under discussion. What are the advantages and disadvantages of writing in this manner?

24 'What's My Name?' and 'War Games' appear to be about boxing and paintballing but they both make serious points about life in America. What are these points and how well are they expressed?

⬭ Speaking and listening work

Further activities

25 Try writing a lively article with a serious point, for instance 'The Serious Side of Ping Pong'.
26 Choose an activity or area of interest you know well and provide some essential background information for an outsider. Perhaps you could write about 'Who's Who in Hip Hop' or 'Essential Facts About Orienteering'.

Kings, Queens and Emperors

In Britain today we can say what we like about the government and the royal family. In November 2000 the *Daily Mirror* carried a headline 'Killer Queen'. In earlier times people were sent to the gallows for less. Those who read on were relieved – or perhaps disappointed – to learn that Her Majesty Queen Elizabeth II had been captured by a telephoto lens in the act of wringing the neck of a pheasant on a shoot on her own land.

Those who criticised the Emperor Nero openly were risking their lives. And neither Fitzstephen (King Henry II) nor Hurault (Queen Elizabeth I) said a word out of line while they were within reach of a sensitive sovereign.

Much more recently, thousands of people have been killed or imprisoned for criticising those in power. See 'Tiananmen Square' on page 145.

'Good Sport at Balmoral' comes from Queen Victoria's own diary. If she presents herself in an unflattering light, that is her own fault. In fact, she comes over as a good-natured if unimaginative soul, devoted to her family. A journalist would probably have written a livelier report of the day's sport, but would a journalist have been such a conscientious queen?

The Emperor Nero

Gaius Suetonius Tranquillus

The Roman author Suetonius (75–150 AD) is credited with many books, including The Physical Defects of Mankind, Methods of Reckoning Time *– and* The Twelve Caesars, *which may be less riveting than some of the others, but which is the only one that has survived. Here Suetonius describes the musical ambitions of the Emperor Nero.*

Music formed part of [Nero's] childhood curriculum and he early developed a taste for it. Soon after his accession,[1] he summoned Terpnus, the greatest lyre-player of the day, to sing to him when dinner had ended, for several nights in succession, until very late. Then, little by little, he began to study and practise himself, and conscientiously undertook all the usual exercises for strengthening and developing the voice. He would lie on his back with a slab of lead on his chest, use enemas and emetics[2] to keep down his weight, and refrain from eating apples and every other food considered damaging to the vocal chords. Ultimately, though his voice was still feeble and husky, he was pleased enough with his progress to nurse theatrical ambitions. His first stage appearance was at Naples, where, disregarding an earthquake which shook the theatre [in fact the theatre collapsed soon after the audience had left], he sang his piece through to the end …

So captivated was he by the rhythmic applause of some Alexandrian sailors from a fleet which had just put in, that he sent to Egypt for more. He also chose a few young knights, and more than 5000 ordinary youths whom he divided into claques[3] to learn the Alexandrian method of applause and provide it generously whenever he sang. [These groups were called the Bees, who made a loud humming sound, the Roof-tiles, who clapped with hollow hands, and the Brick-bats, who clapped with flat hands.]

---

[1] **his accession:** formally becoming Emperor
[2] **enemas and emetics:** medicines to make a person excrete and vomit
[3] **claques:** groups of people hired to applaud

No one was allowed to leave the theatre during his recitals, however pressing the reason, and the gates were kept barred. We read of women in the audience giving birth, and of men being so bored with the music and the applause that they furtively dropped down from the wall at the rear, or shammed dead and were carried away for burial.

Henry II

William Fitzstephen

*Henry II's Chancellor, and later Archbishop of Canterbury, Thomas Becket
(1118–1170), was also his closest friend. In fact, the king chose Becket for
important office because he thought Becket would let him have his own
way. He was mistaken: but that is another story. Here Becket's clerk gives
an eyewitness account of the two friends horsing around.*

When the daily round of business had been dealt with, the king and
Thomas would sport together like boys of the same age, in hall, in
church and while sitting or riding abroad. One day they were riding
together through the streets of London. It was a hard winter and the
king observed an old man approaching, poor and clad in a thin and
ragged coat.

'Do you see that man?' said the king to the Chancellor.

'Yes, I see him,' replied the Chancellor.

'How poor he is, how feeble, how scantily clad!' said the king.
'Would it not be an act of charity to give him a thick warm cloak?'

'It would indeed, and you, O king, ought to have a mind and an eye
to it.'

In the meantime the poor man came up to them. The king and the
Chancellor both stopped. The king greeted him pleasantly and asked
him if he would like a good cloak. The poor man, not knowing who
they were, thought this was a jest and not meant to be taken seriously.

Said the king to the Chancellor, 'You shall have the credit of this act
of charity,' and laying hands on his hood he tried to pull off the cape
the Chancellor was wearing, a new and very good one of scarlet and
grey, which he struggled hard to keep. A great din and commotion then
arose, and the knights and nobles in their train hastened up wondering
what was the cause of this sudden strife between them. But no one
could tell. Both of them had their hands fully occupied, and more than
once seemed likely to fall off their horses.

At last the Chancellor reluctantly allowed the king to overcome him, and suffered him to pull the cape from his shoulders and give it to the poor man. The king then explained what had happened to his attendants. They all laughed loudly, and some offered their own capes and cloaks to the Chancellor. The poor old man walked off with the Chancellor's cape, joyful and rich beyond expectation, and giving thanks to God.

An Audience with Queen Elizabeth I

André Hurault

André Hurault was an ambassador from France. This interview took place in 1597 when the queen was 64. Hurault shows an impressive awareness of fabrics and fashion.

She was strangely attired in a dress of silver cloth, white and crimson, or silver 'gauze', as they call it. The dress had slashed sleeves lined with red taffeta, and was girt about[1] with other little sleeves that hung down to the ground, which she was for ever twisting and untwisting. She kept the front of her dress open, and one could see the whole of her bosom, and passing low, and often she would open the front of this robe with her hands as if she was too hot. The collar of the robe was very high, and the lining of the inner part all adorned with little pendants of rubies and pearls, very many, but quite small. She also had a chain of rubies and pearls about her neck.

On her head she wore a garland of the same material and beneath it a great reddish-coloured wig, with a great number of spangles of gold and silver, and hanging down over her forehead some pearls, but of no great worth. On either side of her ears hung two great curls of hair, almost down to her shoulders and within the collar of her robe, spangled as the top of her head. Her bosom is somewhat wrinkled as well as one can see for the collar that she wears round her neck, but lower down her flesh is exceeding white and delicate, so far as one could see.

As for her face, it is and appears to be very aged. It is long and thin, and her teeth are very yellow and unequal, compared with what they were formerly, so they say, and on the left side less than on the right. Many of them are missing so that one cannot understand her easily when she speaks quickly. Her figure is fair and tall and graceful in whatever she does; so far as may be she keeps her dignity, yet humbly and graciously withal.[2]

---

[1] **girt about:** bound or encircled
[2] **withal:** nevertheless

Good Sport at Balmoral

Queen Victoria

In 1848 Queen Victoria and her husband, Prince Albert, fell in love with the Scottish Highlands in general and Balmoral Castle in particular. In 1868 excerpts from the queen's Balmoral diaries were published. The book became a bestseller.

The extract describes the last day of their holidays, when Albert decided to do some deer stalking.

Monday 11 October 1852

After luncheon, Albert decided to walk through the wood for the last time, to have a last chance, and allowed Vicky and me to go with him. At half-past three o'clock we started, got out at Grant's and walked up part of Carrop, intending to go along the upper path, when a stag was heard to roar, and we all turned into the wood. We crept along, and got into the middle path. Albert soon left us to go lower, and we sat down to wait for him; presently we heard a shot – then complete silence – and, after another pause of some little time, three more shots. This was again succeeded by complete silence. We sent someone to look, who shortly after returned, saying the stag had been twice hit and they were after him. Macdonald next went, and in about five minutes we heard 'Solomon' give tongue, and knew he had the stag at bay. We listened a little while, and then began moving down hoping to arrive in time; but the barking had ceased, and Albert had already killed the stag; and on the road he lay. He was a magnificent animal, and I sat down and scratched a little sketch of him on a bit of paper that Macdonald had in his pocket, which I put on a stone – while Albert and Vicky, with the others, built a little cairn[1] to mark the spot.

We heard, after I had finished my little scrawl, and after the carriage had joined us, that another stag had been seen near the road; and we had not gone far before we saw one below the road, looking so handsome.

---

[1] **cairn:** mound of stones to form a memorial

Albert jumped out and fired – the animal fell, but rose again, and went on a little way, and Albert followed. Very shortly after, however, we heard a cry, and ran down and found Grant and Donald Stewart pulling up a stag with a very pretty head. Albert had gone on, Grant went after him, and I and Vicky remained with Donald Stewart, the stag and the dogs. I sat down to sketch, and poor Vicky, unfortunately, seated herself on a wasp's nest, and was much stung. Donald Stewart rescued her, for I could not, being myself too much alarmed. Albert joined us in twenty minutes, unaware of having killed the stag. What a delightful day!

Activities

Understanding
The Emperor Nero

1 List the exercises Nero undertook to train his voice.
2 Write two brief accounts of a performance by Nero, one for public circulation and one for your own private diary.

Henry II

3 What, according to this passage, was the relationship between Henry and Thomas like? How did they behave together?
4 The relationship between the king and Thomas seems to be equal but what phrase in the passage reveals where the real power lies?

An Audience with Queen Elizabeth I

5 This extract does not tell us directly about Queen Elizabeth's mood but, judging by her actions, how do you think she was feeling during the audience?
6 What effect does the contrast between Elizabeth's rich attire and aged body create?

Good Sport at Balmoral

7 Clearly Queen Victoria would not have been popular with today's anti-blood sports lobby. What attitude does she have towards the dead animals?
8 Queen Victoria writes simply about the events of her day but what evidence is there in the passage that shows that she is a rich and powerful woman?

Style
The Emperor Nero

9 Suetonius does not say how powerful Nero is but demonstrates his power by describing the things he is able to do. Choose one such demonstration, like his employment of over 5000 people to clap his performances, and explain the degree of power and wealth this implies.

Henry II

10 This anecdote from the life of Thomas Becket is told in the style of a fable or fairy story. What fairy-tale elements can you identify?
11 What is the underlying message of this anecdote?

An Audience with Queen Elizabeth I

12 ⌒ Much of the effect of this description is gained from accurate choice of nouns. With a partner go through the passage and identify the adjectives used. What do most of them have in common?

⌒ Speaking and listening work

Good Sport at Balmoral

13 Look at the first sentence. What does it imply about the relationship between Queen Victoria and her husband?

14 This account is written in the first person. What does it tell us of how a queen sees the world?

Speaking and listening
The Emperor Nero

15 ⬭ The Emperor Nero is famous for going mad. With a partner or small group discuss whether you think that being in charge of a huge empire and having almost absolute power drove him mad or whether he was probably mad to start with.

Henry II

16 ⬭ Henry II caused Thomas Becket to be murdered, although he was extremely sorry about it afterwards. Discuss whether you think very powerful people can really have friends.

An Audience with Queen Elizabeth I/ Good Sport at Balmoral

17 ⬭ Queen Elizabeth never married and Queen Victoria was never sure about how much her husband should be involved in affairs of state. Research the extra difficulties that powerful women in the past had to deal with.

Comparisons

18 All four extracts deal with power and wealth. Which of these people do you feel most sympathy towards? Give reasons for your answer.

19 What do the two extracts dealing with male sovereigns have in common? What do the two extracts dealing with queens have in common?

Further activities

20 Imagine you are either Nero, Henry II or Elizabeth I. Using information from the extracts, write about a day in your life in the style of Victoria.

21 Imagine that you could apply for the job of king or queen of England at a certain point in history. Write a letter of application to the Prime Minister explaining why you would make a good queen or king. Show that you have thought about the advantages and disadvantages of the position and mention the personal qualities that you possess that would make you a suitable candidate.

⬭ Speaking and listening work

Plague and Pestilence

The Black Death, the Great Plague of London and the cholera epidemic in Naples are just three of the monstrous epidemics which have claimed the lives of countless millions over the centuries.

Plague and pestilence thrive among dirt and ignorance, polluted water supplies and inadequate sanitation. They murder millions in developing countries; but they lurk much nearer to home too. In the year 2000, over 1000 people died of infections contracted in Britain's hospitals. Plague and pestilence are alive and well, and living near you.

The Black Death

Henry Knighton

The Black Death, which is believed to have originated in India, killed 25 million people in the fourteenth century – about a quarter of the entire population of Europe. By reducing the number of people available to work the land, the Black Death ultimately led to the end of the Feudal System.

The dreadful pestilence penetrated the sea coast by Southampton and came to Bristol, and there almost the whole population of the town perished, as if it had been seized by sudden death; for few kept their beds more than two or three days, or even half a day. Then this cruel death spread everywhere around, following the course of the sun. And there died at Leicester in the small parish of St Leonard more than 380 persons, the parish of Holy Cross, 400; in the parish of St Margaret's, 700; and so in every parish a great multitude.

In the same year there was a great murrain[1] of sheep everywhere in the kingdom, so that in one place in a single pasture more than 5000 sheep died; and they putrefied so that neither bird nor beast would touch them. Everything was low in price because of the fear of death, for very few people took any care of riches or property of any kind. A man could have a horse that had been worth 40 shillings for half a mark, a cow for 12 pence, a heifer for 6 pence, a sheep for 3 pence, a lamb for 2 pence and a large pig for 5 pence.[2] Sheep and cattle ran at large through the fields and among the crops, and there was none to drive them off or herd them; for lack of care they perished in ditches and hedges in incalculable numbers throughout all districts, and none knew what to do.

In the following autumn a reaper was not to be had for a lower wage than 8 pence, with his meals; a mower for not less than 10 pence, with

---

[1] **murrain:** disease
[2] 1 old penny = less than half 1 new penny

meals. Wherefore many crops wasted in the fields for lack of harvesters. But in the year of the pestilence there was so great an abundance of every kind of grain that almost no one cared for it.

The Scots, hearing of the dreadful plague among the English, suspected that it had come about through the vengeance of God. Believing that the wrath of God had befallen the English, they assembled in Selkirk forest with the intention of invading the kingdom, when the fierce mortality overtook them, and in a short time about 5000 perished. As the rest, the strong and the feeble, were preparing to return to their own country, they were followed and attacked by the English, who slew countless numbers of them.

Meanwhile the King sent a proclamation into all the counties that reapers and other labourers should not take more than they had been accustomed to take, under the penalty appointed by statute. But the labourers were so lifted up and obstinate that they would not listen to the King's command, but if anyone wished to have them he had to give them what they wanted, or else lose his fruit and crops or satisfy the lofty and covetous wishes of the workmen.

And when it was known to the King that they had not observed his command, and had given higher wages to the labourers, he levied heavy fines [on the employers]. And afterwards the King had many labourers arrested, and sent them to prison; many withdrew themselves and went into the forests and woods; and those who were taken were heavily fined. Their ringleaders were made to swear that they would not take daily wages beyond the ancient custom, and then were freed from prison. And in like manner was done with the other craftsmen in the boroughs and villages ... After the aforesaid pestilence, many buildings, great and small, fell into ruins in every city, borough and village for lack of inhabitants. Likewise, many villages and hamlets became desolate, not a house being left in them, all having died who dwelt there.

The Great Plague of 1665

Samuel Pepys

From 1 January 1660 until 31 May 1669, when his wife died and his failing eyesight made writing difficult, Samuel Pepys kept a diary. That in itself is fairly unusual – how many people have the self-discipline to write every day for more than nine years? History was in the making: the restoration of the monarchy in 1660, the Great Plague in 1665, the Great Fire in 1666. But the most exciting thing about Pepys's diary is its sheer interest and vitality. Here is that rare thing: an interesting man's chronicles of interesting times.

June 7: The hottest day that ever I felt in my life. This day, much against my Will, I did in Drury Lane see two or three houses marked with a red cross upon the doors, and 'Lord have mercy upon us' writ there – which was a sad sight to me, being the first of that kind that to my remembrance I ever saw.

June 10: In the evening home to supper, and there to my great trouble hear that the plague is come into the City; but where should it begin but in my good friend and neighbour's, Dr Burnett in Fenchurch Street, which troubles me mightily.

June 11: I saw poor Dr Burnett's door shut. But he hath, I hear, gained great goodwill among his neighbours; for he discovered it himself first, and caused himself to be shut up of his own accord – which was very handsome.

June 15: The town grows very sickly, and people to be afeared of it – there dying this last week of the plague 112, from[1] 43 the week before.

June 17: It stroke[2] me very deep this afternoon, going with a hackney coach[3] down Holborn, the coachman I found to drive easily and easily;

---

[1] **from:** compared to
[2] **stroke:** struck
[3] **hackney coach:** horse-drawn carriage for hire

at last stood still, and came down hardly able to stand; and told me that he was suddenly stroke very sick and almost blind, he could not see. So I light[4] and went into another coach, with a sad heart for the poor man and trouble for myself, lest he should have been stroke by the plague.

June 29: To Whitehall, where the Court is full of waggons and people ready to go out of town. This end of the town every day grows very bad of the plague. The Mortality bill[5] is come to 267, which is about 90 more than last week.

July 12: A solemn fast-day for the plague growing upon us.

July 13: Above 700 died of the plague this week.

July 20: 1089 [died] of the plague this week. My Lady Carteret did this day give me a bottle of plague-water.[6]

August 3: I had heard 2010 [had died] of the plague [this week]. Mr Marr [told] me how a maid-servant of Mr John Wrights, falling sick of the plague, was removed to an out-house, and a nurse appointed to look to her[7] – who, being once absent, the maid got out of the house at the window and run away. The nurse coming and knocking and getting no answer, believed she was dead and went and told Mr Wright so; who, and his lady, were in great strait what to do to get her buried. [Mr Wright went to look for someone to bury the maid] but they would not; so he went home full of trouble; and on the way he met the wench walking over the Common, which frighted him worse than before. And was forced to send people to take her, which they did; and they got one of the pest Coaches and put her into it to carry her to a pest-house.

And passing in a narrow lane, Sir Anthony Browne, with his brother and some friends in the coach, met this coach with the Curtains drawn close. The brother being a young man, and believing there might be

---

[4] **light:** got out

[5] **Mortality bill:** total number of dead people

[6] **a bottle of plague-water:** (probably) a liquid made from herbs to keep the disease away

[7] **to look to her:** to look after her

some lady in it that would not be seen, and the way being narrow, he thrust his head out of his own into her coach to look and there saw somebody look very ill, and in a sick dress, and stunk mightily; which the coachman also cried out upon. And presently they came up to some people [who] told [them] that it was a maid of Mr Wright's carried away sick of the plague – put the young gentleman into a fright had almost cost him his life, but is now well again.

Cholera in Naples

Axel Munthe

Axel Munthe was born in Sweden, but he practised as a doctor all over Europe before retiring to an Italian island. Here he built the wonderful villa after which his life story, The Story of San Michele, *first published in 1929, is named. Munthe was on holiday in Lapland when he saw a headline in a copy of* The Times *that an English visitor had left behind:* TERRIBLE OUTBREAK OF CHOLERA IN NAPLES; OVER A THOUSAND CASES A DAY. *An hour later Munthe was on his way to Italy to do what he could to help.*

My offer to serve on the staff of the cholera hospital of Santa Maddalena was accepted. Two days later I vanished from the hospital having discovered that the right place for me was not among the dying in the hospital, but among the dying in the slums.

How much easier it would have been for them and for me, thought I, if only their agony were not so long, so terrible! There they were lying for hours, for days, cold as corpses, with wide-open eyes and wide-open mouths, to all appearances dead and yet still alive. Did they feel anything, did they understand anything? So much the better for the few who could still swallow the teaspoonful of laudanum[1] one of the volunteers rushed in to pour into their mouths. It might at least finish them off before the soldiers and the half-drunk beccamorti[2] came at night to throw them all in a heap in the immense pit on the Composanto dei Colerosi. How many were thrown in there alive? Hundreds, I should say. They all looked exactly alike, I myself was often unable to say if they were dead or alive. There was no time to lose, there were dozens of them in every slum, the orders were strict, they all had to be buried in the night.

As the epidemic approached its climax I had no longer any reason for complaining that their agony was so long. Soon they began to fall

---

[1] **laudanum:** medicine made from opium

[2] **beccamorti:** corpse collectors

down in the streets as if struck by lightning, to be picked up by the police and driven to the cholera hospital to die there a few hours later. The cabby who drove me in the morning in tearing spirits to the convict prison of Granatello, near Portici and was to take me back to Naples, was lying dead in his cab when I came to look for him in the evening. Nobody wanted to have anything to do with him in Portici, nobody wanted to help me to get him out of the cab. I had to climb on the box to drive him back to Naples myself. Nobody wanted anything to do with him there either, it ended by my having to drive him to the cholera cemetery before I could get rid of him.

Often when I returned in the evening to the locanda,[3] I was so tired that I threw myself on the bed as I was, without undressing, without even washing myself. What was the good of washing in this filthy water, what was the good of disinfecting myself when everybody and everything around me was infected, the food I ate, the water I drank, the bed I slept in, the very air I breathed! Often I was too frightened to go to bed, too frightened to be alone. I had to rush out into the street again, to spend the remainder of the night in one of the churches. There were plenty of churches to sleep in when I dared not go home. All the hundreds of churches and chapels in Naples were open the whole night, ablaze with votive candles and thronged with people.

But it was not only of the cholera I was afraid. I was also terrified from first to last of the rats. They seemed just as much at home in the slums as the wretched human beings who lived and died there. To be just, they were on the whole inoffensive and well-behaved rats, at least with the living, attending to their business of scavengers, handed over to them since the time of the Romans, the only members of the community who were sure to get their fill. They were as tame as cats and almost as big. Once I came upon an old woman, nothing but skin and bones, almost naked, lying on a rotten straw mattress in a semi-dark sort of grotto. I was told she was the 'vavama', the grandmother. She was paralysed and totally blind and had been lying there for years. On the filthy floor of the

---

[3] **locanda:** inn

cave sat on their haunches, half-a-dozen enormous rats in a circle round their unmentionable morning meal. They looked quite placidly at me, without moving an inch. The old woman stretched out her skeleton arm and screamed in a hoarse voice: 'pane![4] pane!'

But when the sanitary commission started on its vain attempt to disinfect the sewers, my fear grew into terror. Millions of rats who had been living unmolested in the sewers since the time of the Romans, invaded the lower part of the town. Intoxicated by the sulphur[4] fumes and the carbolic acid,[5] the rats rushed about the slums like mad dogs. They did not look like any rats I had ever seen before. They were quite bald with extraordinarily long red tails, fierce blood-shot eyes and pointed black teeth. If you hit them with your stick, they would turn round and hang onto the stick like a bull-dog. Never in my life have I been so afraid of any animal as I was of these mad rats, for I am sure they were mad. Over a hundred severely bitten men, women and children were taken to the Pelligrini hospital the very first day of the invasion. Several small children were literally eaten up.

I shall never forget a night in a fondaco in Vicolo della Duchessa. The room, the cave is a better word, was almost dark, only lit up by the little oil lamp before the Madonna. The father had been dead for two days but the body was still lying there under a heap of rags. I was sitting on the floor by the side of the daughter, beating off the rats with my stick. She was already quite cold, she was still conscious. I could hear the whole time the rats crunching at the body of the father. At last it made me so nervous that I had to put him upright in the corner like a grandfather clock. Soon the rats began again eating ravenously his feet and legs. I could not stand it any longer. Faint with fear I rushed away.

---

[4] ***pane:*** bread
[5] ***sulhpur/carbolic acid:*** chemicals used for disinfecting the sewers

Activities

Understanding
The Black Death

1 Draw a sketch map of England and mark on it the places mentioned in the first paragraph. Given that the plague spread along trade routes mark a likely route for its spread.

2 Briefly describe the main economic effects of the Black Death.

The Great Plague of 1665

3 How did ordinary people find out about the seriousness of the plague at any given point?

4 Pepys is interested in how individuals behaved during the plague. In general, does he take an optimistic or a pessimistic view of human nature? Give reasons for your answer.

Cholera in Naples

5 Why do you think Axel Munthe left the hospital to go and work in the slums?

6 How did fear of cholera in and around Naples affect people's behaviour towards each other?

7 Describe the religious and medical responses to the epidemic.

8 What was Munthe's greatest terror during the cholera epidemic?

Style
The Black Death

9 Why do you think the passage gives so much space to arrangements for confession and absolution of sins as opposed to, say, arrangements for stopping the spread of the disease?

10 What evidence is there, in the choice of material and the views expressed, that this is an official account of the Black Death? Use quotations to support your answer.

The Great Plague of 1665

11 Look at how Pepys expresses his feeling in these extracts. Do you get a good impression of how he really felt or do you think he is understating how he felt?

12 Reread the account of events of 3 August again. How does this description differ from the majority of entries in the extract? How much of it did Pepys see with his own eyes?

Cholera in Naples

13 This passage contains sections which deal with the epidemic in general terms and sections which give very particular accounts of single incidents. Which type of writing gives the best impression of what the epidemic was like? Give reasons for your answer.

14 Choose an account of a single incident, such as the starving old woman or the attack of the rats. How does Axel Munthe make these incidents so horrific?

Speaking and listening

15 ⌂ Imagine that your group are members of the council of a town just outside London or Naples. Plague has broken out in the city and you have a choice of sending help or closing the town to all strangers. Stage your discussion at a time when no one in your community has fallen ill but remembering that if the plague does break out you will probably need help from outside too.

16 ⌂ Discuss the plagues and epidemics that threaten us today, such as AIDS, meningitis, influenza and CJD. Apart from our medical knowledge, are we any better off than our ancestors when it comes to dealing with them?

Comparisons

17 Which of these three accounts gives the best sense of what it might be like to live through a plague epidemic? Give reasons for you answers.

Further activities

18 Investigate and define the difference between a plague and an epidemic.

19 Most modern plagues take place away from the public view in hospitals and infirmaries. The epidemics described here have a very real impact on everyday life. Write the script for a television news report on one of these epidemics.

⌂ Speaking and listening work

Hot and Cold

Some people talk of global warming, with huge areas of Britain under water, while others say we are in for a new Ice Age. Here John Evelyn describes the big freeze of 1684, when the sap froze and split the trees, and ships were trapped in the ice. His diary records the terrible hardship and loss of life, but also the carnival atmosphere on the frozen River Thames.

What sticks most in your mind about Samuel Pepys's description of the Great Fire of London? The cowardly Lord Mayor? The looting, or the poor pigeons with their singed wings? Or maybe it is Pepys's unquenchable optimism and zest for life: 'However, we had an extraordinary good dinner, and were as merry as at this time we could be.'

Life goes on, in spite of everything fate and the elements can throw at us.

The Great Fire of London

Samuel Pepys

Samuel Pepys was born in London in 1633 and died in 1703. He was an excellent organiser and has been described as 'the first modern civil servant'. But it is for his diary that Pepys is famous.

From 1660 until 1669, when failing eyesight forced him to give it up, he reported the great historical events of the day as well as his own adventures. Here he writes about the Great Fire of London (1666), said to have started in Pudding Lane and ended at Pie Corner. If you have visited London you may have passed a tall pillar with golden flames on top. This pillar, known simply as The Monument, commemorates the Great Fire of London.

September 2 (Sunday)

I was called up at about three in the morning to hear of a great fire in the City. So I rose, and slipped on my night-gown, and went to the window; but I thought it far enough off; and so went to bed again, and to sleep. About seven I rose again to dress myself, and there looked out of the window, and saw the fire not so much as it was, and further off … By and by Jane comes and tells me that she hears that above 300 houses have been burnt down by the fire we saw, and that it is now burning all Fish-street, by London Bridge.

So I made myself ready and walked to the Tower[1] and got up upon one of the high places. There I did see the houses at the end of the bridge all on fire, and an infinite great fire on this and the other side of the bridge; which made me anxious about poor Michell and Sarah who live on the bridge.

So down I went with my heart full of trouble to the Lieutenant of the Tower, who told me that the fire had begun this morning in the King's baker's house in Pudding Lane, and that it had burned down St Magnes Church and most of Fish Street already. So I went down to the

---

[1] **Tower:** Tower of London

water-side, and there got a boat, from which I saw a lamentable fire. Poor Michell's house was already burned, and the fire running further, so that it got as far as the Steel-yard while I was there. Everybody was endeavouring to remove their goods, flinging them into the river, or into lighters[2] that lay off. Some poor people were staying in their houses until the fire touched them, and then running into boats, or clambering from one pair of stairs by the water-side to another. And the poor pigeons were unwilling to leave their houses, but hovered about the windows and balconies, till they burned their wings, and fell down.

And so I stayed, and in an hour's time saw the fire rage every way, and nobody to my sight endeavouring to quench it, but instead removing their goods and leaving all to the fire. Having seen it get as far as the Steel-yard, and the wind mighty high, and driving it into the City; and everything after so long a drought proving combustible, even the very stones of the churches, I went to White Hall. There people came and I gave them an account which dismayed them all, and word was carried in to the King.

So I was called for, and did tell the King and the Duke of York what I had seen, and said that unless His Majesty commanded houses to be pulled down, nothing could stop the fire. They seemed much troubled, and the King commanded me to go to the Lord Mayor on his behalf, and command him to spare no houses, but to pull them down [to make a clear space in the path of the fire]. The Duke of York told me to tell the Lord Mayor that he could have all the soldiers he needed.

Pepys hurried to deliver these messages to the Lord Mayor.

... At last I met the Lord Mayor in Canning-street, like a man spent,[3] with a handkerchief about his neck. To the King's message he cried, like a fainting woman, 'Lord! what can I do? I am spent; people will not obey me. I have been pulling down houses; but the fire overtakes us faster than we can do it.' He said he needed no more soldiers; and that

---

[2] **lighters:** boats for carrying goods
[3] *spent:* exhausted

he himself needed to refresh himself, having been up all night. So he left me, and I him, and walked home. I saw people almost distracted, and no manner of means used to quench the fire.

The houses were very close together, and full of matter for burning, such as pitch and tar in Thames Street, and warehouses full of oil and wines and brandy and other things. And I saw people filling the churches with their goods, when they themselves should have been quietly there at this time.

By this time it was about twelve o'clock, so I went home, and there I found my guests ... We were in great trouble and disturbance about this fire, not knowing what to think of it. However, we had an extraordinary good dinner, and were as merry as at this time we could be.

After dinner ...

... I met with the King and the Duke of York in their barge and went with them to Queenhith. Their order was to pull down houses apace; but little could be done, for the fire was approaching so fast. There were hopes of stopping it at the Three Cranes above the bridge, and at Buttolph's Wharf below the bridge, but the wind carried the fire into the City. The river was full of lighters and boats taking in goods, and goods swimming in the water. I now went to White Hall, and from there walked to St James's Park, and there met my wife and Creed and Wood and his wife, and walked to my boat. Then we took to the water again. The fire was still increasing and the wind was great. All over the Thames, with our faces in the wind, we were almost burned with the shower of fire-drops.[4] This is very true; so as houses were set alight by these drops and flakes of fire, three or four, even five or six houses away from one another.

When we could endure no more upon the water, we went to a little alehouse on the Bankside near the Three Cranes, and there stayed till it was almost dark. We saw the fire grow, and as it grew darker, the fire appeared more and more, and in corners and upon steeples, and between churches and houses, as far as we could see up the hill of the

---

[4] **fire-drops:** sparks

City, in a most horrid malicious bloody flame, not like the fine flame of an ordinary fire. We stayed until, it being darkish, we saw the fire as only one entire arch of fire from this to the other side of the bridge, and in a bow up the hill above a mile long; it made me weep to see it. The churches and houses all on fire, and all flaming at once; with the horrid noise of the flames and the cracking of houses at their ruin. So we went home with a sad heart.

Poor Tom Hater came with very few of his goods saved out of his house, which was burned upon Fish Street Hill. I invited him to sleep at my house, and did receive his goods; but news came that the fire was spreading, so we were forced to pack up our own goods and prepare for their removal. So by moonlight we carried much of my goods into the garden, and Mr Hater and I removed my money and iron chests into my cellar, thinking that the safest place. We got my bags of gold into my office, ready to carry away, and my chief papers of accounts also. We put Mr Hater to bed for a while, but he got very little rest, for there was so much noise and commotion ...

September 4
... I wrote to my father this night, but the post-house being burned, the letter could not go.

The Great Frost Fair

John Evelyn

The diarist John Evelyn lived and wrote around the same time as Samuel Pepys. Here he describes the antics when the River Thames was frozen.

January 24 1684

The frost still continuing more & more severe, the Thames before London was planted with bothes[1] in formal streetes, as in a City, or Continual faire, all sorts of Trades & shops furnished, and full of Commodities, even to a Printing presse, where the People & Ladys tooke a fansy to have their names Printed & the day & yeare set downe, when printed on the Thames. This humour tooke so universaly, that 'twas estimated the Printer gained five pound a day, for printing a line onely at six-pence a Name, besides what he gott by Ballads.

Coaches now plied from Westminster to the Temple, & from several other staires[2] too & froo, as in the streetes; also on sleds, & sliding with skeetes.[3] There was likewise Bull-baiting, Horse & Coach races, Pupet-plays & interludes,[4] Cookes & Tipling & lewder places; so as it seemed to be a bacchanalia,[5] Triumph or Carnoval on the Water, whilst it was a severe Judgement upon the Land: The trees not onely splitting as if lightning-strock, but Men & Cattell perishing in divers[6] places, and the very seas so locked up with yce, that no vessells could stirr out, or come in. The fish & birds, & all our exotique Plants & Greenes universaly perishing; many Parks of deere were destroyed, & all sorts of fuell so deare that there were greate Contributions to preserve the poore alive; nor was this severe weather much lesse intense in most parts of

[1] ***bothes***: booths
[2] ***staires***: stages
[3] ***skeetes***: skates
[4] ***interludes:*** short, dramatic entertainments
[5] ***bacchanalia:*** drunken festival
[6] ***divers:*** various

Europe, even as far as Spain, the most southern tracts. London, by reason of the excessive coldnesse of the aire hindring the ascent of the smoke, was so filld with the fuliginous[7] steame of the Sea-Coale, that hardly could one see crosse the streete, & this filling the lungs with its grosse particles exceedingly obstructed the breast, so that one could scarce breath. There was no water to be had from the Pipes & Engines, nor could the Brewers, and divers other Tradesmen work, & every moment was full of disastrous accidents, etc.

January 30
The frost still raging as fircely as ever, the River of Thames was become a Camp, ten thousands of people, Coaches, Carts, & all manner of sorts continuing & increasing: miserable were the wants of poore people, Deere universaly perished in most of the parks thro-out England, & very much Cattell.

February 4
I went to Says-Court to see how the frost & rigorous weather had dealt with my Garden, where I found many of the Greenes & rare plants utterly destroied; The Oranges & Myrtils very sick, the Rosemary & Lawrell dead to all appearance, but the Cypresse like to indure it out: I came to London the next day when it first of all began to Thaw, and pass'd over without alighting in my Coach from Lambeth to the Horse-ferry at Mill-bank at Westminster; the Weather growing lesse severe, it yet began to freeze againe; but there was first a Map or Landskip[8] cut in copper representing all the manner of the Camp, & the several actions, sports and passe-times thereon in memory of this signal Frost.

---

[7] **fuliginous:** sooty
[8] **Landskip:** landscape

Activities

Understanding
The Great Fire of London
1   What was Pepys's initial reaction to the fire?
2   How did most people respond as the fire approached?
3   What part did Pepys play in the fight against the fire?

The Great Frost Fair
4   List some of the activities that took place on the River Thames during the fair.
5   Which activity seems to have struck John Evelyn as the most unusual?
6   What other effects did the Great Frost have, apart from freezing the River Thames?

Style
The Great Fire of London
7   Was this account written on the days that are described or several days or weeks later? What clue about when the account was written can you find in the first paragraph?
8   How can you tell that this is an extract from a private diary rather than an account intended for publication? Describe some of the features that give you this impression, and support your views with quotations.

The Great Frost Fair
9   John Evelyn's *Diary* is usually quite personal but in this extract he provides a report of the Frost Fair. Look carefully at the account and try to decide how much of what he reports he saw himself. Why do you think he chose to write in this way on this occasion?
10 What techniques does John Evelyn use to make up his description? (Hint: look carefully at his use of nouns and adjectives.)

Speaking and listening
11 ⬭ Have you ever kept a diary? With a partner, discuss what kind of events you recorded. Did you ever write about a major public event?
12 ⬭ If you have never kept a diary discuss with your partner what you would be most interested in recording. Would you comment in your diary about major public events?

⬭ Speaking and listening work

Comparisons

13 Answer the following questions as fully as you can, giving examples where appropriate:
   • Which diary entry gives the clearest overview of the events described?
   • Which gives the most vivid picture? Which of the two approaches do you prefer?
   • Is it possible to be closely involved in events and understand what is going on at the same time?

Further activity

14 Either rewrite Evelyn's account to give a better idea of his feelings, or rewrite Pepys's account so that it gives a more general picture.

Executions and Funerals

Reportage majors in death: battles, epidemics, natural disasters, executions, funerals and the final moments of the famous. In this section are a deathbed, two executions and a royal funeral.

This chapter would not be complete without at least one execution. For a long time executions took place in public, supposedly to serve as a dreadful warning. In fact people flocked to the free entertainment and fought for souvenirs.

King Louis XVI of France was not the only king to be beheaded for treason (Charles I of England was executed by order of Parliament in 1649), but he *was* the only king to be guillotined. Joseph Ignace Guillotin was a leading light of the French revolution. He did not invent the decapitating device which made him famous – it had been used earlier in Germany and Italy – but he was the one who, in 1791, had it adopted by the Revolutionary government to clear the backlog of condemned 'traitors' quickly and supposedly humanely.

Joan, later Saint Joan, of Arc was burnt to death: not by the English for defeating them in battle (although being thrashed by a teenage girl must have been humiliating), but by a church court of the Inquisition for heresy – unorthodox religious beliefs. She was canonised – declared a saint – in 1920.

Not all royal events are as meticulously organised or as decorous as the ones we are accustomed to seeing on television. In his diary Horace Walpole describes King George II's funeral: a solemn ceremony which dissolved into slapstick comedy.

The Execution of King Louis XVI of France

Abbé Edgworth

King Louis XVI was found guilty of treason against his country and condemned to death. An Irish priest, the Abbé Edgworth, travelled with the king in the coach that took him to the scaffold on 21 January 1793.

The coach arrived, amid a great silence, and stopped in the middle of a wide empty space which had been left round the scaffold; this space was edged with cannon, and beyond, as far as the eye could reach, was an armed multitude.

As soon as the king felt the coach coming to a stop, he leaned over to me and said in a whisper: 'We have arrived, if I am not mistaken.' My silence said yes. One of the executioners came forward to open the door of the coach, but the king stopped him and, putting his hand on my knee, said to the gendarmes:[1] 'Messieurs, I commend this gentleman to your care; be good enough to see that after my death he is not offered any insult; I charge you to see to this.' As the gendarmes did not reply, the king began to repeat it in a louder voice, but he was interrupted by one of them saying: 'Yes, yes, we'll take care of that; leave it to us.' I must add that he said it in a tone of voice which would have frozen me, if at such a moment it had been possible for me to think for myself.

As soon as the king got out of the coach, three of the executioners surrounded him, and tried to remove his outer garments. He pushed them away with dignity, and took off his coat himself. He also took off his collar and his shirt, and made himself ready with his own hands. The executioners, disconcerted for a moment by the king's proud bearing, recovered themselves and surrounded him again in order to bind his hands.

'What are you doing?' said the king, quickly drawing his hands back.

'Binding your hands,' answered one of them.

---

[1] **gendarmes:** police officers

'Binding me!' said the king in a voice of indignation. 'Never! Do what you have been ordered, but you shall never bind me.'

The executioners insisted; they spoke more loudly, and seemed about to call for help to force the king to obey.

This was the most agonising moment of this terrible morning; one minute more, and the best of kings would have received an outrage a thousand times worse than death, by the violence that they were about to use towards him. He appeared to fear this himself, and turning his head, seemed to ask my advice. At first I remained silent, but when he continued to look at me, I said, with tears in my eyes, 'Sire, in this new outrage I see one last resemblance between Your Majesty and the God Who is about to be your reward.'

At these words he raised his eyes to heaven with an expression of unutterable sadness. 'Surely,' he replied, 'it needs nothing less than His example to make me submit to such an insult.' Then, turning to the executioners: 'Do what you will; I will drink the cup, even to the dregs.'

The steps of the scaffold were extremely steep. The king was obliged to lean on my arm, and from the difficulty they caused him, I feared that his courage was beginning to wane; but what was my astonishment when, arrived at the top, he let go of me, crossed the scaffold with a firm step, silenced with a glance the fifteen or twenty drummers who had been placed directly opposite, and in a voice so loud that it could be heard as far away as the Font Tournant, pronounced these unforgettable words: 'I die innocent of all the crimes with which I am charged. I forgive those who are guilty of my death, and I pray God that the blood which you are about to shed may never be required of France.'

Two days after his death, France and Britain were at war.

The Execution of Joan of Arc

Jean Massieu

Joan of Arc (born in 1412 and burnt as a heretic in 1431) was one of the most influential women of all time. In an era when men went to war and women stayed at home, Joan led an army against the English. Here the usher Jean Massieu describes Joan's last moments.

With great devoutness she asked to have the cross. Hearing that, an Englishman who was present made a little cross of wood from the end of a stick, which he gave her and devoutly she received and kissed it, making pious lamentations to God our Redeemer who had suffered on the Cross for our redemption, of which Cross she had sign and representation.

And she put this cross into her bosom, between her flesh and her clothes, and furthermore asked humbly that I enable her to have the cross from the church so that she could have it continually before her eyes until death. And I so contrived that the parish clerk of Saint-Sauveur brought it to her. Which being brought, she embraced it long and closely and retained it until she was bound to the stake. Brother Isambart had gone with the parish-clerk to fetch the cross. The pious woman asked, requested and begged me, as I was near her at her end,[1] that I would go to the nearby church and fetch the cross to hold it raised right before her eyes until the threshold of death, that the cross which God hung upon should be continually before her eyes in her lifetime.

Being in the flames she ceased not until the end to proclaim and confess aloud the holy name of Jesus, imploring and invoking without cease the help of the saints in paradise. And what is more, in giving up the ghost and bowing her head, she uttered the name of Jesus as a sign that she was fervent in the faith of God.

---

[1] **end:** death

The Funeral of George II

Horace Walpole

George II died in 1760. The Dukes of Cumberland and Newcastle were sons of the king.

When we came to the chapel of Henry VII, all solemnity and decorum[1] ceased – no order was observed, people sat or stood where they could or would, the yeomen of the guard were crying out for help, oppressed by the immense weight of the coffin, the Bishop read sadly, and blundered in the prayers.

The real serious part was the figure of the Duke of Cumberland, ... [in] a cloak of black cloth with a train of five yards. Attending the funeral of a father, how little reason soever he had to love him, could not be pleasant. His leg extremely bad, yet forced to stand upon it near two hours, his face bloated and distorted with his late paralytic stroke, which has affected too one of his eyes, and placed over the mouth of the vault into which, in all probability, he must himself so soon descend – think how unpleasant a situation! He bore it all with a firm and unaffected countenance.

This grave scene was fully contrasted by the burlesque[2] Duke of Newcastle – he fell into a fit of crying the moment he came into the chapel and flung himself back in a stall, the Archbishop hovering over him with a smelling-bottle – but in two minutes his curiosity got the better of his hypocrisy and he ran about the chapel with his glass to spy who was or was not there, spying with one hand and mopping his eyes with t'other.

Then returned the fear of catching cold, and the Duke of Cumberland, who was sinking with heat, felt himself weighed down, and, turning round, found it was the Duke of Newcastle standing upon his train to avoid the chill of the marble.

---

[1] **decorum:** correct behaviour
[2] **burlesque:** ridiculous

It was very theatric to look down into the vault, where the coffin lay, attended by mourners with lights. Clavering, the Groom of the Bedchamber, refused to sit up with the body, and was dismissed by the King's order.

Activities

Understanding
The Execution of King Louis XVI of France

I Explain as fully as you can why Louis XVI finally agreed to have his hands bound.

2 What impression does this account give of the character of King Louis? Give reasons for your answer.

The Execution of Joan of Arc

3 What use does Joan of Arc make of the three crosses mentioned in this account?

4 As Joan was being burned as a heretic (someone who disagrees with the doctrine of the Church) she might have been expected to reject Jesus and the cross as she died. What does this account imply about the justice of putting her to death?

The Funeral of George II

5 What discomforts did the Duke of Cumberland have to put up with at his father's funeral?

6 Judging from his adverse comments about people's behaviour how does Horace Walpole think people *should* behave at funerals?

Style
The Execution of King Louis XVI of France

7 What is the Abbé Edgworth's attitude towards the king? Support your opinion with quotations.

The Execution of Joan of Arc

8 This account focuses on Joan of Arc's pious behaviour. Why do you think Jean Massieu was more interested in this than, say, her personal feelings or her physical suffering?

The Funeral of George II

9 This account could be described as tragi-comic. What are the comic elements and what are the tragic ones?

Speaking and listening

10 ⬭ With a partner or in a small group discuss whether you think it is *ever* right for the state to put an individual to death.

Comparisons

11 In the two accounts of executions the observers are clearly biased. What indications of bias can you find? Does it matter if an account is biased as long as we, as readers, are aware of it?

12 Of the three deaths described which is the most moving? Give reasons for your opinion.

Further activity

13 All people facing death by execution have time to reflect on their lives: what they have achieved, what they will miss, what they have enjoyed, and what they regret. Write down your thoughts about these aspects of your own life.

Speaking and listening work

Prisoners

All these stories are told in the first person: 'I was there.' All survived their imprisonment and lived to taste freedom again. On reading the extracts you might wish to ask 'How on earth did they live from day to day without giving up hope or losing their mind?'

Job Hortop's bald account of his experiences gives nothing away. His matter-of-fact description of the hunger and hardship, lashings and lice, makes his tale all the more horrifying. In the case of Mayhew's nameless returned convict, sheer stubborn bloodymindedness seems to have kept him going.

Harry Keith was in the men's camp, as far out of reach of his wife Agnes and son George as if he were on the Moon. Agnes celebrated George's birthday by offering the precious gift of an egg to every child in the camp. And her Japanese captors gave her the finest present of all: a visit from her husband.

Leslie Hill escaped from a prisoner of war camp and got clean away, only to find that the 'safe' addresses he had been given were a trap. He was clever enough not to fall into the trap himself, but was afraid that other escapers would get caught – unless he warned them. Hill had the courage to give himself up to the Gestapo in the hope of returning to his PoW camp with the bad news. Lesser men would have gone home anyway, and sent their mates a postcard.

Sentenced to the Galleys

Job Hortop

John Hortop sailed with Sir John Hawkins to the West Indies in 1567. After many hair-raising adventures he and several others were taken prisoner by the Spaniards. Hortop was sentenced to ten years in the galleys.

I with the rest were sent to the galleys, where we were chained four and four together. Every man's daily allowance was 26 ounces of coarse, black biscuit and water, our clothing for the whole year two shirts, two pairs of breeches of coarse canvas, a red coat of coarse cloth, soon on and soon off, and a gown of hair with a friar's hood. Our lodging was on the bare boards and banks of the galleys, our heads and beards were shaven every month; hunger, thirst and stripes we lacked none, till our several times[1] expired.

And after the time of twelve years, for I served two years above my sentence, I was sent back to the Inquisition House in Seville, and there [I was sent to] the everlasting prison remediless.[2]

After a further eleven years Hortop escaped by boat ...

We met an English ship, the galleon *Dudley*, who brought me to Portsmouth where they set me on land the 2nd day of December last past, 1590 ... Thus, having truly set down unto you my travels, misery and dangers, endured for twenty-three years, I end.

---

[1] **times:** sentences
[2] **remediless:** with no chance of appeal

A Returned Convict

Henry Mayhew

At the time Henry Mayhew was published (1852), the law sentenced many convicted criminals to be transported to the penal colony of Van Dieman's Land, which is now Tasmania, instead of a term in one of Britain's overcrowded prisons. Convicts were often held for long periods in prison hulks: time which did not count as part of their sentence. Once they reached Van Dieman's Land, life was very harsh. Mayhew says: 'This man stated that the severity of the Government in this penal colony was so extreme, that men thought little of giving others a knock on the head with an axe, to get hanged out of the way.'

I was sentenced to 14 years' transportation. I was ten weeks in the *Bellerophon* hulk at Sheerness, and was then taken to Hobart Town, Van Dieman's Land, in the *Sir Godfrey Webster*. At Hobart Town sixty of us were picked out to go to Launceston. There we lay for four days in an old church, guarded by constables; and then the settlers came there from all parts, and picked their men out. I got a very bad master. He put me to harvest work that I had never seen before, and I had the care of the pigs [that were as fierce] as wild boars. I then worked in a Government potato-field; in the Government charcoal-works for about 11 months; and then was in the Marine department, going by water from Launceston to George Town, taking Government officers down in gigs,[1] provisions in boats, and such-like.

All the time I consider I was very hardly treated. I hadn't clothes half the time, being allowed only two slop-suits[2] in a year, and no bed to lie on when we had to stay out all night with boats. With 12 years' service at this my time was up, but I had incurred several punishments before it was up. The first was 25 lashes, because a bag of flour had been burst, and I picked up a capful.

---

[1] *gigs:* small boats
[2] *slop-suits:* official issue suits

The flogging is dreadfully severe, a soldier's is nothing to it. I once had 50 lashes, for taking a hat in a joke when I was tipsy; and a soldier had 300 the same morning. I was flogged as a convict, and he as a soldier; and when we were both at the same hospital after the flogging, and saw each other's backs, the other convicts said to me, 'You've got it this time'; and the soldier said, when he saw my back, 'You've got it twice as bad as I have.' 'No,' said the doctor, 'ten times as bad – he's been flogged; but you, in comparison, have only had a child's whipping.'

The cats[3] the convicts were then flogged with were each six feet long, made out of the log-line[4] of a ship of 500 tons burden; nine over-end knots were in each tail, and nine tails whipped at each end with wax-end. With this we had half-minute lashes; a quick lashing would have been certain death. One convict who had 75 lashes was taken from the triangles to the watch-house in Launceston, and asked if he would have some tea – he was found to be dead. The military surgeon kept on saying in this case, 'Go on, do your duty.' I was mustered there, as was every hand belonging to the Government, and saw it, and heard the doctor.

When I was first flogged, there was an inquiry among my fellow-convicts, as to 'How did [he] stand it – did he sing?' The answer was, 'He was a pebble'; that is, I took my flogging like a stone. I said to myself, 'I can take it.' I could have taken the flogger's life at the time, I felt such revenge. Flogging always gives that feeling; I know it does, from what I've heard others say who had been flogged like myself.

In all I had 875 lashes at my different punishments. I used to boast of it at last. I would say, 'I don't care, I can take it till they see my backbone.' After a flogging I've rubbed my back against a wall, just to show my bravery like, and squeezed the congealed blood out of it. Once I would not let them dress my back after a flogging, and I had 25 additional [strokes] for that.

---

[3] **cats:** whips
[4] **log-line:** rope used for measuring the ship's speed

At last I bolted to Hobart Town, 120 miles off. There I was taken before the magistrate, himself a convict formerly; but he was a good man to a prisoner. He ordered me 50, and sent me back to Launceston. At Launceston I was 'fullied'[5] by a bench of magistrates, and had 100 [6] Seven years before my time was up I took to the bush. I could stand it no longer, of course not. In the bush I met men with whom, if I had been seen associating, I should have been hanged in any slight charge.

We do not know how he managed to get back to Britain. Mayhew says: 'I am not at liberty to continue this man's statement at present; it would be a breach of the trust he reposed in me.'

---

[5] **fullied:** fully committed
[6] **100:** 100 strokes

Escape and Recapture

Leslie Hill

There are many stories of daring escapes from prisoner of war camps during World War Two (1939–1945), but this one, which has never appeared in print before, is special. Lieutenant Leslie Hill, MC, escaped from Oflag VIIIF, a PoW camp in Germany. Thanks to his perfect German and good Czech, he reached Prague, where he had been given the addresses of three contacts. These he was instructed to check out, to prepare the ground for a later mass escape.

Hill did as he was told, but found to his dismay that two of the addresses simply did not exist. A sixth sense warned him not to try the third address. Later he was proved right: the third address was a trap. Hill could have got clean away, but instead he chose to get himself recaptured in order to warn his friends.

After the war he was an interpreter during the Nuremburg War Trials – but that, of course, is another story.

I decided that I had to get back to our camp to warn my friends. It was a heartrending decision to have to make, but I could see no alternative. I stood on a small bridge over a stream and dropped my German money into it. I also tore my identity card up and scattered the pieces on the water. Finally I walked into the Czech Police Headquarters.

'I'm an escaped British PoW,' I said to the surprised Czech police sergeant at the charge desk, 'and I've come to give myself up. I'm footsore, hungry, cold and tired (all of which were true – I had big blisters on both my feet), and I've walked all the way from Moravska Trebova and can't go any further.'

The Czech police were extremely kind and friendly. At first they did not really want to know anything about me. In fact, I got the impression that they were thinking of helping me to continue my escape. But then a German police officer, who was obviously attached to the HQ to keep an eye on the Czechs there, came in, and the game was up. However, the Czech policemen managed to get permission from this sour-looking

German creature to give me a really good hot meal, for which I was extremely grateful.

After an hour, I was told that I was to be taken to another town, Kolin, which was some miles away. I supposed that that was where I would be taken back to Oflag VIIIF from. One of the kindly Czech policemen who had fed me was to accompany me.

When we reached Kolin, the policeman took me to a forbidding grey building which was the local prison.

'You'll be all right here,' he told me with a reassuring smile. 'The Czech prison guards will treat you well, and you'll soon be back in your PoW camp with your friends.'

We climbed the stairs, floor after floor, and came to the top. There was a big steel grille across the entrance to that floor, and the word GESTAPO[1] above it. 'Look,' I said to my escort, my heart in my boots.

'Don't worry,' he said with another charming smile, and it occurred to me that he had probably been stringing me along the whole time to keep me quiet on the trip.

A few minutes after my arrival, the local Gestapo chief arrived too, beaming all over his plump red face at the news that he had a British officer in his prison. He was hot and puffing after hurrying up the stairs. When he arrived, my search and interrogation began.

'How did you get out of your camp?' the Gestapo man began.

'I climbed the wire at night,' I answered, putting on an execrable[2] German accent and pretending to be a stupid, harmless idiot.

'And why did you give yourself up?'

'Because I walked the whole way from Mährisch Trubaü, and I was cold, hungry, tired and had blistered feet.' I took off my boots and socks and then said, 'Could I please have a doctor to treat them?'

I could see that the Gestapo chief was frankly incredulous about my version of my escape from the camp, but that he accepted the rest of my story quite happily.

---

[1] **Gestapo:** secret state police

[2] **execrable:** extremely bad

'Why didn't you ask for help from the Czechs?' he asked slyly.

'I kept right away from the people,' I answered. 'They'd have been afraid to help me even if they'd wanted to, wouldn't they?'

He beamed all over his fat red little face and answered, 'Yes, you're quite right. Most of the Czechs are very happy under our strict but just rule. They have work and bread. And those who are not happy dare not do anything about it.' He smirked in a self-satisfied way.

'Why are you not wearing your identification tags?' he asked at last. 'Do you realise that there is nothing on you that can prove that you are really an escaped British prisoner of war? In fact, I could have you shot as a spy!' He smiled triumphantly.

'Well,' I answered, looking as stupid as I could, 'I took off my tags to have my hot shower before I left the camp, and I forgot to put them on again – but look, I'm wearing British boots!' I showed them to him with a look of simulated triumph in my eyes.

He laughed scornfully and said, 'We'll check on your story. Meanwhile, you'll stay with us.'

The chief jailer then took my glasses, my belt and my boots away and led me to the last cell but one on that floor. He unlocked the door after sliding a steel cover off a spyhole in it and looking through. He told me to go in, and as the door opened, five men in scruffy clothes stood to attention in the cell, and one of them said, 'Zelle 5, fünf Männer!' ('Cell No. 5, five men!'). I went in.

The jailer went out, locking the door again, and the five crowded round me and began asking me questions. I knew that any of them might be stool pigeons,[3] so I did not tell them anything I did not want the Germans to know. They asked me for news about the war, but I told them only what I had read in the German papers.

The five were political prisoners, taken by the Gestapo and held in this prison before being sent to Prague for interrogation, or to concentration camps in Germany. They were naturally frightened and uncertain of their fate. Some had already been in concentration camps before.

---

[3] **stool pigeons:** police informers

There were six palliasses[4] on the floor of the cell, which was only built to accommodate two prisoners, and there was a lavatory and wash-basin in one corner. Anyone who wanted to relieve himself had to do it in public.

Night came, and we bedded down. Then began a hammering on the pipes of the wash-basins throughout the prison (the lower floors were ordinary civil ones) which mystified me until I realised that the prisoners were communicating in code. Two or three times the bad-tempered SS man opened the door and shouted to us to stop the noise, but there was really nothing he could do about it, because as soon as the door rattled, the banging in our cell stopped. I presume that information of my arrival in the prison was passed on in this way.

The next morning, we were each brought a bowl of ersatz[5] coffee made from roasted acorns, and a small hunk of dry bread. A few minutes later, the head guard came in and told me to follow him. 'Well, this is it,' I thought, but he only took me to the next cell, the last in the corridor. It was empty except for a bed and the inevitable lavatory and wash-basin.

'We've had orders from higher up to keep you away from the others,' the SS man said, and left me alone in the cell.

So began two weeks of solitary. I was not allowed to have anything to read, I was not allowed to lie down during the day, there was nothing to look at, as there was only one small, heavily barred window high up in one wall, I had to clean the place myself, including the lavatory, once a day, and I had to stand at attention and say, 'Zelle 6, ein Mann' whenever any of the guards came in. I protested about the cleaning and standing at attention, saying that as a British officer I should not have to do these things, but I was roughly told that, as a Gestapo prisoner, I had no rights. Realising that, if I continued my pretence of being a harmless, rather stupid fellow, there would be more chance of my getting back to Oflag VIIIF, I did not make an issue of these things.

The light in the cell would be put on from time to time during the

---

[4] **palliasses:** straw-filled mattresses

[5] **ersatz:** imitation

night, from outside, and an eye would appear at the spy-hole, checking that I was not trying to dig my way out.

Once a week, I could hear the other prisoners being taken out into an exercise yard, cell by cell, to walk round for half an hour, but I was not included. Once a week, too, they were taken down to the ground floor for a hot shower, and this I was included in, although I had to go alone. All prisoners were supposed to provide their own soap, but as mine soon ran out, and I had no money to buy more, I was given a piece by one of the guards. During my weekly shower period, I was also given back my razor so as to have a shave.

Food was brought three times a day by one of the prisoners, a tall, gaunt Czech who was obviously a 'trusty'. We soon became very friendly. He would give me extra pieces of bread and extra large helpings of the thin soup which, with the bread, constituted our midday meal (the other two were 'coffee' and a little more of the coarse bread). He did more to keep up my morale than anyone else in that grim place.

A few days later I was allowed to join the half-hour exercise in the yard with the inmates of the next-door cell. We went round and round in the fresh air, and I could see the green copper dome of a church over the high wall at one end of the yard. It was wonderful.

The rest of the time I had nothing to occupy me except my thoughts. I was not allowed to sleep during the day. I tried making up crossword puzzles in my head, but it was difficult to remember the other words while one was working on a new one. I tried various children's games, like thinking of animals, towns, insects etc. beginning with A, B, C etc. right through to Z. I tried tracing routes in great detail, e.g. the one from my college at Cambridge to the boathouse. I tried remembering poems I had learnt by heart at various periods of my life: anything to keep my brain active and sane.

After I had been in that cell five weeks, I said to the head guard one day, 'You know, I think I'm beginning to go mad, sitting in here with nothing to do or look at day after day. Couldn't I at least have a book to look at?'

He was sympathetic. 'I'll see what I can find,' he said. He went out and came back with two small paperbacks in German. One was a school text dealing with symbiosis, I remember.

I devoured the little books eagerly, learning more about the ways of pilot fish, sharks, egrets and rhinoceroses than I had ever known before.

A few days later the head guard came in with my glasses, boots and belt. 'Put these on,' he said. 'You're leaving.'

Hill was taken to Oflag 79 in Brunswick, 24 hours' train journey away.

At the camp, I was taken in to see the Deputy Commandant and the Security Officer, whom I recognised at once. I had come to the camp I had been in before I had escaped, only now it had been moved to the centre of Germany, and had had its name changed.

The German officers interrogated me in the presence of the policeman. 'How did you escape?' asked the fat, red-faced Deputy Commandant.

I repeated my story about climbing the wire.

The Security Officer smiled nastily and said, 'Actually, we know how you escaped. You waited until the side gate was open for the changing of the guard, and then one of you, dressed as a German, marched the rest, dressed as Russians, out. The German corporal who let you through was severely beaten up and put in prison.'

'I sentence you to 10 days in cells for escaping and having civilian clothes,' the Deputy Commandant said to me.

'But I've already done six weeks in cells!' I protested.

'We have no cognisance[6] of that,' he answered. 'You were outside the jurisdiction[7] of the German Army. In fact, you are very lucky to be back.' (It was not until I got back to the camp that I realised how lucky I had been: the big escape from the RAF camp had taken place at about

---

[6] **cognisance:** knowledge

[7] **jurisdiction:** power

the same time as ours, and over 40 of the escapers had been shot on Hitler's orders.)

At first I was given German officers' food from their mess, which was incredibly good compared with what I had lived on for the past six weeks, but then the camp was informed of my return, and food was sent in from the Oflag 79 mess, together with my battledress. Also I was given letters and a book which had arrived for me during my absence. It was a Czech grammar, which I had asked for long ago through the Red Cross. The Security Officer brought it to me personally, and grinned sardonically as he handed it over. 'A bit too late, eh?' he said.

George's Birthday

Agnes Newton Keith

From 1942 to 1945 Agnes Newton Keith, her husband Harry and their little son George were among thousands of innocent civilians who were interned by the Japanese. Agnes and George were in one part of the camp with the women and children, Harry was in the men's camp, and they seldom saw each other.

George had his third birthday, and his first one in captivity, shortly after our arrival at Kuching. On the strength of its being his birthday, I obtained an unusual concession from Lieutenant Nekata, who permitted me to purchase thirty-four eggs through the canteen, one egg for each child now in camp. I sold a dress to get the money, and I paid twenty-five cents per egg. On his birthday morning George distributed an egg to every child with birthday greetings.

At nine o'clock we were sent for and told to come to the Japanese offices. Here we found Harry waiting in the next room. Lieutenant Nekata told me to my surprise that we were permitted to have an interview.

Harry and I had not met since leaving Berhala. We looked at each other, and again we were speechless. This time we could not even touch hands. Then Harry held out his arms for George, and when he had his arms round him it seemed he could not let him go.

I asked Harry if he had asked for the interview. He said no, that he had been working in the fields when he was called to the office. When he arrived Nekata said, 'Today is your son's birthday. You may see wife and child.' Evidently my request to Nekata to buy eggs for George's birthday had been noted. I did not know how to account for this kindness, especially to me, except that sometimes the Japanese were kind. We had half an hour to talk, then said good-bye.

George liked my presents least of all, they being necessities. I made him two pairs of pants, cut from the bottom of the old blue gingham counterpane that I had used to bundle our blanket roll in, and a baju and sarong to sleep in, cut from the bottom of my rose kimono. The Oriental effect was more to his taste than were the blue gingham pants.

Penelope made him a Tom Sawyer rag doll out of scraps from her clothing, stuffed with cotton from her pillow. Tom had a fishing rod and line with a fish attached. Marjorie North made him a small pillow covered with a piece of her dress and stuffed with rags, also two tiny wool golliwogs riding in a newspaper boat. Tony gave him pictures cut out of an old newspaper, Pete and Frankie gave him two lumps of sugar, the last of the supply their mother brought into camp. Alastair and David and Derek gave sago-flour biscuits, and Edith and Eddie Cho gave three rusks, the last of Mrs Cho's tinful that she brought in a year ago. Susan gave a blue elephant that Babs Hill had made out of the end of Susie's blanket. The greatest luxury was a tiny cake of soap from 'Auntie May', as there was no more soap to be had in camp.

George went to bed very happy. He would not have liked his presents any more if they had cost a lot of money. He was so good that he wasn't spanked all day, a fact worthy of mention. I went to bed happy, having seen Harry.

Activities

Understanding
Sentenced to the Galleys
1   What do you think was the worse aspect of life on the galleys? Give reasons for your answer.

A Returned Convict
2   List some of the work that the convict had to do during his time in Van Dieman's Land.
3   The convict says of his flogging, 'I used to boast of it'. What do you think this shows about him and the conditions which he survived?

Escape and Recapture
4   What reason did Leslie Hill give for giving himself up?
5   What were Hill's main concerns after his recapture? How did he behave in order to achieve his goals?

George's Birthday
6   How would you describe Agnes's and Harry's response to their unexpected meeting? How did George help them?
7   What do the presents that George received tell you about life in the camps?

Style
Sentenced to the Galleys
8   Job Hortop does not record his feelings about life on the galleys but his choice of nouns and the order in which he presents them gives some indication of his emotions. Comment briefly on the way Hortop's account is organised and what this shows.

A Returned Convict
9   What use does Henry Mayhew make of direct quotation? How does this help to give an impression of the life described?
10 Does the use of colloquial expressions in this extract make it seem more authentic or more difficult to understand? Support your answer with quotations.

Escape and Recapture
11 Compare the way in which Leslie Hill describes the Czech and German policemen in the third paragraph. What does his choice of words indicate?
12 Hill's account seems to have been written at some distance in time from the events described. What evidence is there of this in the text?

George's Birthday

13 Very few mothers would remember every single birthday gift given to their child. How does the fact that Agnes Newton Keith remembers her son's gifts in detail help to make her account more vivid and convincing?

Speaking and listening

Sentenced to the Galleys

14 🗩 Remind yourself of the conditions that Job Hortop endured in the galleys for twelve years and of the punishment that the convict suffered. With a partner, discuss how the two men might have found the strength to survive.

15 🗩 Organise a 'balloon debate' in which the survivor is the prisoner who suffered most. Four volunteers could describe their sufferings in the role of the four prisoners mentioned here and the rest of the class could vote on who should be allowed to stay in the balloon.

Comparisons

16 Compare the behaviour of the Czech, German and Japanese guards in the second two extracts. Does it surprise you that the prisoners can speak positively of their guards?

17 Look again at the suffering in these accounts. In your opinion, which is harder to endure, physical or mental pain? Use quotations from the texts to back up your ideas.

18 In the first two accounts the men feel the need to show how tough they are. What kind of bravery is shown in the second two accounts?

Further activities

19 Imagine that you are a prisoner of war separated from your loved ones. Write a letter to a friend or a family member which describes your life and how you feel. How truthful would you be about your suffering?

20 There have been many films made about escapes from prison. Design a poster and write the script for a trailer of a film featuring any one of the prisoners in this section. Think about the images you would use in the poster, the scenes you would include in the trailer and the information you would provide.

🗩 Speaking and listening work

Innocent Blood

More death, more bloodshed. This section is about people murdered for reasons of race or religion. Adolf Hitler blamed the Jews for all Germany's woes, and six million Jews were killed during the Second World War: shot, gassed, beaten, starved to death, experimented on without anaesthetics, in the name of ethnic cleansing.

'Ethnic cleansing' implies that some races are unclean, unfit to live, and they must be scrubbed away. In the 1990s a million men, women and little children were slaughtered in Rwanda for belonging to the 'wrong' tribe. Read Andrew Moir's description of land mines in Bosnia, specially designed to attract little children; and the heart-breaking words of a child attacked in a German park in 1998 for being a Romany.

The shedding of innocent blood has a long and infamous tradition. When the Three Wise Men told King Herod that a king had been born in Bethlehem, the king ordered what has become known as the Massacre of the Innocents:

> Then Herod, when he saw that he was mocked of the wise men, was exceeding wroth, and sent forth, and slew all the children that were in Bethlehem, and in all the coasts thereof, from two years old and under.

Matthew 2: 16–18

1940s: Genocide in the Ukraine

Hermann Graeb

Genocide is defined as 'the deliberate extermination of a race or other group'. During the Second World War six million Jews were systematically slaughtered. Hermann Graebe gave this evidence at a trial shortly after the end of the war.

I drove to the site, accompanied by my foreman, and saw near it great mounds of earth, about thirty metres long and two metres high. Several trucks stood in front of the mounds. Armed Ukrainian militia drove the people off the trucks under the supervision of an SS man. The militia men acted as guards on the trucks and drove them to and from the pit. All these people had the regulation yellow patches on the front and back of their clothes and thus could be recognised as Jews. My foreman and I went directly to the pits. Nobody bothered us.

Now I heard rifle shots in quick succession from behind one of the earth mounds. The people who had got off the trucks – men, women and children of all ages – had to undress upon the orders of an SS man, who carried a riding or dog whip. They had to put down their clothes in fixed places, sorted according to shoes, top clothing and underclothing. I saw a heap of shoes of about 800 to 1000 pairs, great piles of underlinen and clothing.

Without screaming or weeping these people undressed, stood around in family groups, kissed each other, said farewells, and waited for a sign from another SS man, who stood near the pit, also with a whip in his hand. During the fifteen minutes that I stood near I heard no complaint or plea for mercy.

I watched a family of about eight persons, a man and a woman, both about fifty, with their children aged about one, eight and ten, and two grown-up daughters of about twenty to twenty-four. An old woman with snow-white hair was holding the one-year-old child in her arms and singing to it and tickling it. The child was cooing with delight. The couple were looking on with tears in their eyes. The father was holding the hand of a boy about ten years old and speaking to him softly, the boy was fighting his tears. The father pointed to the sky, stroked his head and seemed to explain something to him.

At that moment the SS man at the pit shouted something to his comrade. The latter counted about twenty persons and instructed them to go behind the earth mound. Among them was the family which I have mentioned. I well remember a girl, slim and with black hair, who as she passed close to me, pointed to herself and said, 'Twenty-three.'

I walked around the mound and found myself confronted by a tremendous grave. People were closely wedged together and lying on top of each other so that only their heads were visible. Nearly all had blood running over their shoulders from their heads. Some of the people shot were still moving. Some were lifting their arms and turning their heads to show that they were still alive. The pit was already two thirds full. I estimated that it already contained about 1000 people.

I looked for the man who did the shooting. He was an SS man, who sat at the edge of the narrow end of the pit, his feet dangling into the pit. He had a tommy-gun[1] on his knees and was smoking a cigarette.

The people, completely naked, went down some steps which were cut in the clay wall of the pit and clambered over the heads of the people lying there, to the place to which the SS man directed them. They lay down in front of the dead or injured people; some caressed those who were still alive and spoke to them in a low voice. Then I heard a series of shots ...

The next batch was approaching already. They went down into the pit, lined themselves up against the previous victims and were shot. When I walked back round the mound I noticed another truckload of people which had just arrived. This time it included sick and infirm persons. An old, very thin woman with terribly thin legs was undressed by others who were already naked, while two people held her up. The woman appeared to be paralysed. The naked people carried the woman around the mound. I left with my foreman and drove back to Dubno.

---

[1] **tommy-gun:** Thompson sub-machine-gun

1990s: Genocide in Rwanda

Fergal Keane

Fergal Keane is a prize-winning BBC journalist who has reported from many of the world's worst trouble spots. In 1994 he reported from Rwanda in Africa, shortly after up to a million people from the Tutsi tribe were put to death by members of a rival tribe, the Hutus, in a hundred-day orgy of murder and torture. Here he and his team, together with Rwandan drivers and soldiers, arrive at the scene of a massacre beside a church.

We bounce and jolt along the rutted track on an evening of soft, golden light. The air is sweet with the sound of warm savannah grass. Clouds of midges hover around the cars, dancing through the windows. We are exhausted and hungry from the day's travelling, and we are too tired to bother fighting off the insects.

Up ahead is the façade[1] of a church built from red sandstone. 'This is Nyarubuye,' says Frank. Moses begins to slow the car down and Glenn is preparing his camera to film.

As we drive closer, the front porch of the church comes into view. There is a white marble statue of Christ above the door with hands outstretched. Below it is a banner proclaiming the celebration of Easter, and below that there is the body of a man lying across the steps, his knees buckled underneath his body and his arms cast behind his head. Moses stops the car; but he stays hunched over the wheel and I notice that he is looking down at his feet.

I get out and start to follow Frank across the open ground in front of the church. Weeds and summer grasses have begun to cover the gravel. Immediately in front of us is a set of classrooms and next to that a gateway leading into the garden of the church complex. As I walk towards the gate, I must make a detour to avoid the bodies of several

---

[1] **façade:** front

people. There is a child who has been decapitated and there are three other corpses splayed on the ground.

Frank lifts a handkerchief to his nose because there is a smell unlike anything I have ever experienced. I stop for a moment and pull out my own piece of cloth, pressing it to my face. Inside the gate the trail continues. The dead lie on either side of the pathway. A woman on her side, an expression of surprise on her face, her mouth open and a deep gash on her head. She is wearing a red cardigan and a blue dress, but the clothes have begun to rot away, revealing the decaying body underneath.

I must walk on, stepping over the corpse of a tall man who lies directly across the path, and feeling the grass brush against my legs, I look down to my left and see a child who has been hacked almost into two pieces. The body is in a state of advanced decay and I cannot tell if it is a girl or a boy. I begin to pray ... prayers I have not said since my childhood, but I need them now.

We come to an area of wildly overgrown vegetation where there are many flies in the air. The smell is unbearable here. I feel my stomach heave and my throat is completely dry. And then in front of me I see a group of corpses. They are young and old, men and women, and they are gathered in front of the door of the church offices. How many are there? I think perhaps a hundred, but it is hard to tell. The bodies seem to be melting away. Such terrible faces. Horror, pain, fear, abandonment. I cannot think of prayers now. Here the dead have no dignity. They are twisted and turned into grotesque shapes, and the rains have left pools of stagnant, stinking water all around them.

They must have fled here in a group, crowded in next to the doorway, an easy target for the machetes and the grenades. I look around at my colleagues and there are tears in the eyes of our sound recordist, Tony. Glenn is filming, but he stops every few seconds to cough. I stay close to our team leader David Harrison, a BBC producer with long experience of Africa, because at this moment I need his age and strength and wisdom. He is very calm, whispering into Glenn's ear from time to time with suggestions, and moving quietly. The dead are everywhere.

We pass a classroom and inside a mother is lying in the corner surrounded by four children. The chalk marks from the last lesson in mathematics are still on the board. But the desks have been upturned by the killers. It looks as if the woman and her children had tried to hide underneath the desks. We pass around the corner and I step over the remains of a small boy. Again he has been decapitated. To my immediate left is a large room filled with bodies. There is blood, rust-coloured now with the passing weeks, smeared on the walls. I do not know what else to say about the bodies because I have already seen so much.

David and the crew have gone into the church and I follow them inside, passing a pile of bones and rags. There are other bodies between the pews and another pile of bones at the foot of the statue of the Virgin Mary, next to the holy water fountain, a man lies with his arms over his head. He must have died shielding himself from the machete blows.

'This is unbelievable,' whispers Tony into my ear. We are all whispering, as if somehow we might wake the dead with our voices.

Outside the church the night has come down thick and heavy. Tony shines a camera light to guide our way. Even with this and the car lights I nearly trip on the corpse of a woman that is lying in the grass. Moths are dancing around the lights as I reach the sanctuary of the car.

While we are waiting for Glenn and Tony to pack the equipment away, we hear a noise coming from one of the rooms of the dead. I turn to Moses and Eduard. 'What is that?' I ask.

'It is only rats, only rats,' says Moses. As we turn to go, we look back and in the darkness see the form of the marble Christ gazing down on the dead. The rats scuttle in the classrooms again.

Later Keane discovers how the killers were able to identify Tutsis, as opposed to members of other tribal groups, in order to murder them.

That night we arrive at the office of the Bourgmestre[2] of Rusomo, Sylvestre Gacumbitsi. He has fled to Tanzania along with the Hutu

---

[2] **Bourgmestre:** mayor

population of the area. The building has several offices and also houses a health centre.

The building has sustained almost no war damage, and the rebels have not looted the stores of medical and office equipment. Most poignantly, in a room at the very back is a library of index cards. These are in fact the identity cards of every local resident. There are thousands of these thin paper cards on to which are fixed the photographs of the bearers. Each card is marked with the name, address and ethnic identity of the resident, Hutu, Tutsi, Twa or other. Dust has gathered on the cards, and when I flick through it rises up and stings my eyes and nose. The colonial government introduced this system of population registration and their Rwanda Hutu successors entrenched it as a means of political control ...

These cards have been used as instruments of genocide.[3] With the ethnic identity and address of every resident registered here at the commune building, the Interahamwe had a ready-made death list.

I look at face after face of Tutsis and wonder if any are still alive. Anybody who imagines that the killing was an arbitrary and disorganised tribal bloodbath had better come here. I have no doubt that this is an index list for murder, prepared years in advance and held in readiness for the day when the Tutsis might need to be sorted out.

---

[3] **genocide:** deliberate killing of a particular race or group of people

1998: Land Mines in Bosnia

Andrew Moir

Flight Lieutenant Andrew Moir is not a full-time serviceman. He has a demanding job in Customs and Excise; but he gives up his free time to serve as an officer in the Royal Air Force Volunteer Reserve. His duties – sometimes dull, sometimes dangerous – take him to the world's trouble spots. Here he talks about his experiences in Bosnia in May and June 1998.

I found Bosnia full of contradictions. It was hot and humid during the day and cold at night; it also rained heavily day and night. I saw the remains of communist rule: bland, functional concrete buildings that would not look out of place in Basildon or Milton Keynes; but there were also some very picturesque places with old public buildings, churches and mosques. The countryside was very varied too. On the journey from Sarajevo to Banja Luka the scenery changed from 'flat and farmed', by way of rolling, wooded hillsides to rugged mountains and glens like my native Scotland. If only the inhabitants could stop being anti-social with each other, I thought, they could make a fortune from tourism.

But not yet awhile. The roadsides were littered with wrecked cars, buses and trucks, the result of a combination of careless driving, drink driving, enemy action and the roads themselves. Badly made in the first place and very neglected since, they were full of potholes and worse.

I was on patrol with the Royal Military Police contingent of SFOR (Stabilisation FORce). One of my duties was helping to distribute a Serbo-Croat publication called *Bridges*. The aim of course was to bring people together. Call it propaganda if you like; I can't argue about that. Everything in *Bridges* was supposed to be true, but I can't confirm that, as I don't read Serbo-Croat.

Reactions to our magazine varied. Many people would come up and ask for a copy. Maybe they read it eagerly from cover to cover; maybe they just wanted it for the crossword. Other people would take copies and crumple them up in front of us, to make a point.

We also handed out crayons and colouring books to the children. This was not just good PR: it was a matter of life and death. These colouring books taught the children about land mines. You know the sort of thing: 'There are six teddy bears hidden in this picture. Find them and colour them in', 'Join the dots to find three farmyard friends', or 'Draw a line under the odd one out'. Our colouring books set similar tasks, except that here the name of the game was 'Spot the Land Mines'.

There are six million land mines in Bosnia that we know of; and God knows how many more that we are unaware of. Documentation is pitifully scanty. When the warring factions were laying land mines, the information about their locations and numbers was seldom documented. Whoever had laid them would know all about them, which was fine if he was still around. Often, of course, he had been killed, or posted elsewhere, and the information was lost.

Most land mines are meant to be inconspicuous. They are, after all, designed as traps for the unwary. Obviously, if you are walking across a field and you see a suspicious-looking object on the ground, you tend to avoid it. But in Bosnia, as well as laying conventional land mines, both sides laid mines which were intended to be noticed. The chilling thing about them was their appearance. These mines were disguised as little dolls and toy cars. You can imagine what happened next.

In safer places, we teach our kids to keep out of danger: walk on the footpath, don't take sweets from strangers. We do not need to teach them to beware of land mines, any more than we need to teach them not to pat strange elephants. For children in Bosnia mine awareness is all too relevant. Curiosity killed the cat. Never pick anything up unless you know where it came from, unless you want to be a statistic.

A statistic? In Disneyland Paris they are constructing a path from the car park to the theme park entrance. Each small hexagonal paving stone is engraved with the name of a visitor to the theme park who has paid handsomely to commemorate a happy day out. Thousands of visitors have sponsored their paving stones, but it is a couple of hundred yards from car park to theme park and it will be a while before the path is finished. Meanwhile, there is a wall in Zagreb, more than five feet high and hundreds of yards long; and every brick is engraved with a name of someone who died in the conflict in Croatia. That wall has made me realise why SFOR has to be there: to ensure there are no more bricks in that wall – and no more walls.

1990s: A Good Refugee

Anonymous

From a leaflet issued by the Refugee Council in London

I am a seven years old girl from Poland. I am not like any other seven-year-old. I am a gypsy. I crawl for I can't walk. I came to England with my dad. My mum is still in a German hospital. Some men attacked me and my mum in the park. When I woke up in the hospital my right leg below the knee was missing. The men in the park cut it off. The fingers of my right hand were also cut off. I do not know the reason. I will try to be a good refugee here in England. I would love to see mum. I would like to have a bigger pushchair and learn to write with my left hand. And I promise to be a good refugee.

Activities

Understanding
1940s: Genocide in the Ukraine

1   In note form outline how the Jewish people of the Ukraine were 'processed' from arrival to death.
2   How would you describe the behaviour of the Jews as they waited to die?

1990s: Genocide in Rwanda

3   Look at the description in paragraph two. How does it change as it progresses? What is the effect of this movement on the reader?
4   Judging from their remains, how had most of the people in the extract been killed?
5   How did the group of journalists react to what they found?

1998: Land Mines in Bosnia

6   Why did the army hand out crayons and colouring books to the children?
7   What does the fact that some land mines were designed to look like dolls or toy cars tell you about the motives of the people who planted them?

1990s: A Good Refugee

8   How much understanding of what has happened to her does the girl show? Does this make her words more or less powerful? Give reasons for you answer.

Style
1940s: Genocide in the Ukraine

9   Most of this description is a single paragraph. Why do you think the author has chosen not to break up his narrative into separate paragraphs?
10 The only feeling of his own that Herman Graeb records is surprise that he was not ordered away. He also says little about the feelings of the people either killing or being killed. Instead he records what he saw people doing. Is this technique more or less effective than if he had stated how evil the killers were or how dignified the victims were? Give reasons for your opinion.

1990s: Genocide in Rwanda

11 This account is written in the present tense. Why do you think Fergal Keane has chosen this tense for his account?
12 Keane does record his own feelings and reactions, as well as those of other witnesses. However, towards the end he says, 'I do not know what else to say about the bodies because I have already seen so much.' Describe the progress of his feelings and say whether you think their inclusion makes his account more or less shocking.

1998: Land Mines in Bosnia

13 What does Andrew Moir's description of the road to Disneyland add to this account? Can you find other examples where he uses comparisons from 'our' world? What effect do the comparisons have?

14 The final paragraph begins with a sentence which is not, strictly speaking, a sentence. It is very short and is in the form of a question. How well does this work as an introduction to the final paragraph?

1990s: A Good Refugee

15 Much longer descriptions could have been chosen for this advertisement. Why do you think this short letter was chosen?

16 What effect does using the 'voice' of a seven-year-old have on the impact of the crimes committed?

Speaking and listening

17 ⌒ The extract by Fergal Keane is from a book called *Letter to Daniel*. It is primarily written for the author's son. Discuss with a partner or small group whether children should be exposed to the horrors that are described in this section or whether they should be protected from them.

18 ⌒ Holocaust Day has been introduced to remind people of the killing of six million Jews during the Second World War. Discuss with a partner why you think the world should remember the Holocaust. What does the fact that we have set up such a day say about our attitudes to genocide?

Comparisons

19 ⌒ With the exception of a few comments in Herman Graeb's account, all of these reports focus on victims. Is it possible to understand the view of those who commit genocide? Discuss with a partner why it is important to bear witness to the kinds of horrors that are described in these accounts and how they might be useful in preventing them happening again.

20 The Jewish and Rwandan accounts could be dismissed by some as from another time and in a far off place. How do 'Land Mines in Bosnia' and 'A Good Refugee' try to bring the issues closer to home?

Further activities

21 Death brings an end to suffering but life can be difficult for those who survive. Devise an advertisement asking for support for survivors of genocide or war. Think about how you will gain your audience's attention and whether you want to shock them into action or engage their sympathies.

22 Write down your thoughts on why it is important to know about humanity's worst crimes.

⌒ Speaking and listening work

Crowds

The *Collins Cobuild English Dictionary*, which is intended for students of English as a foreign language, defines a crowd as 'a large group of people who have gathered together, for example to watch or listen to something interesting, or to protest about something'.

The gathering together is the important thing. Why do television commentators say, 'The audience/crowd *is* going wild' as 1000 concert-goers applaud or 50 000 Man. United fans wave their scarves in the air at the same moment? Surely it is because a great many individuals are acting as one. A wit once described a crowd as 'a life form with a thousand heads and no brain'. Not true! A crowd has a thousand brains, all concentrating on the same thing. Put a thousand music-lovers, each with individual thoughts, hopes and fears, into a concert hall, and they become an audience, united in their enjoyment of the music. During the interval they become individuals again, gossiping, consulting their programmes, buying drinks from the bar or queuing for the lavatories. Then the bell goes for the second half of the performance and the thousand concert-goers become an audience again.

Here, then are four crowds: two unbearably tragic, one almost jolly (what do *you* think of a government that sets a timetable for different protest groups?) and finally a joyous carnival at which, to repeat the well-worn cliché, 'the crowd went wild'.

Disaster at Hillsborough

David Miller

Times *reporter David Miller specialises in sports reports. On 17 April 1989, Miller went to Sheffield's Hillsborough stadium in the full expectation of seeing Nottingham Forest play Liverpool in an FA Cup semi-final.*

With disbelieving eyes, we sat in the grandstand and watched almost 100 people die in front of us at an FA Cup semi-final.

For a whole hour or more, from the time the match was halted after six minutes by a policeman coming onto the pitch to instruct the referee to remove the players, we were captive witnesses, and partly accomplices, to a tragedy that is a consequence of collective incompetence in the organisation of a sporting event.

Even as the game kicked off, circumstances were accelerating during a period of only a few minutes towards inescapable disaster, as a bedlam of people funnelled into a tunnel feeding the terrace behind the Liverpool goal: a tunnel from which there was no retreat backwards, and no safety valve at the front end. These were not hooligans, nor were they, as at Heysel, the victims of mindless rivalry. They died, innocent white figures prostrate on the green grass from whom the breath of life had been crushed, because of the fences built to restrain the mounting hooliganism of the past 25 years.

This was not like Heysel, where we watched incandescent[1] Liverpool spectators charge at Italians, and drive them into a corner where a wall collapsed. The Heysel disaster arrived after a long and avoidable overture of threats on the terraces, and in its awfulness was quite quickly over.

The Hillsborough slaughter had a sudden, swift arrival; and then a drawn-out macabre climax that was initially unapparent to Nottingham Forest supporters at the opposite end. They began by booing what they supposed was Liverpool hooliganism, and was in fact mortal agony.

---

[1] **incandescent:** raging

We watched them die because the South Yorkshire police, with tragically misplaced good intention, opened the gates at the northern, Leppings Lane, end of Hillsborough stadium, thereby sending a torrent of spectators into an already dangerously overcrowded central terrace behind the goal.

We watched them die because police, in scheduling their control of an identical fixture to last year, were more concerned with traffic flow outside the ground before and afterwards – to have Forest at the larger southern Kop end near to the M1 – than with accommodation inside the ground.

Down at the front of the terrace, young people were crushed against barriers with a force exceeding half a tonne, yet for five or ten minutes it looked no more, from 50 yards away, than another crowd becoming restive as the match began. Steel fences buckled as they died.

Down on the pitch, as I moved among the carnage after the game had been halted, I saw mature policemen, sweat-stained in shirt sleeves from their efforts to relieve the victims and to bring back to life the lifeless, crying unashamedly at the hopelessness of a disaster that had overwhelmed them.

We watched them die on this black Saturday because the ambulances which arrived were too few and already too late; because the firemen and police could not reach the majority of the victims being trampled on underfoot, on account of the high, so-called safety fence separating them from the pitch; and because Hillsborough, a modernised but still old-fashioned ground, had little if any of the necessary life-saving equipment.

One of the police, who had been vainly pumping on motionless chests and attempting the kiss of life, said despairingly: 'I had two of them just go on me as I tried. One of them seemed to start breathing again, but there was no oxygen available.'

Those who did not die, and were not either weeping at the loss of friends or limp with shock and pain, were angry. A group of them surrounded me, supposing me to be an official, and eventually had to be restrained by a policewoman as they made hysterical accusations to me against the FA and Sheffield Wednesday authorities for disproportionate ticket allocation, and the police for opening the gates.

'They only care about the money,' a Liverpool spectator screamed at me, a man about 30 and tidily dressed but trembling with fear and frustration. 'They waved us through the gate, and there was already no bloody room in there. The police on the other side of the fence [by the pitch] were yelling at us to move back, but that was impossible. We were out of control. We are human. We've behaved ourselves ever since Heysel, but they go on treating us like animals.' Spectators in the three unaffected grandstands sat through the drama as though watching some horror movie. Bobby Robson, the England team manager, twisted and turned in his director's-box seat in evident torment.

Yet anyone who saw the scenes immediately before the start of the match, outside at the Leppings Lane end, know that the police, including several on horseback, were rapidly losing control of a hoard of spectators aggressively pressing towards the turnstiles, with and without tickets.

No one wanted to take responsibility on this terrible day. Inquiries will be painfully revealing. Mr Peter Wright, the Chief Constable of South Yorkshire, was almost incoherent at the press conference after the full impact of the horror had become apparent. There was no evidence of any connection, he insisted, between the opening of the gates at the back and the pulverising of bodies at the front. It was a truth he simply could not bring himself to acknowledge.

Dr John Williams, a London University lecturer who has specialised in a study of crowd behaviour, had seen the near-impossible congestion in the street leading to B turnstile. Why, he asks, had the police not done more to reduce this surge?

As police and firemen and ground stewards still struggled to free the trapped and the dying from the terraces, some 15 minutes after the game had halted, I climbed the steps of the police viewing turret.

From this position it must have been apparent, shortly before the start of the match, that congestion was already intolerable immediately behind the Liverpool goal. Why was there not closer radio co-ordination between police inside and those who took the decision to open the gates, so releasing a fresh river into the flooded arena?

The Chief Constable says there was danger to life in the mounting pressure that was building up outside. If the police could not control the crowd in the open, had they the right to believe the crisis would be solved by pouring people indiscriminately into the stadium? No one can judge with hindsight what was the correct course in the minutes before the disaster became unavoidable.

Those trying to cope, desperate and powerless police sergeants, waitresses from the stadium restaurant with pathetic jugs of fresh water moving tearfully from casualty to casualty, firemen who had never seen corpses on such a scale, were also suffering a day they will never forget.

Tiananmen Square

John Simpson

There are two kinds of protester in this piece: the violent ones, who throw petrol bombs at army vehicles, and the others, who sing the Internationale and campaign peacefully for a better, fairer way of life. The tragedy is that the Chinese government used tanks against both kinds of protester.

We set out for Tiananmen Square. A cyclist rode past, shouting and pointing. What it meant we couldn't tell. Then we came upon a line of soldiers. Some of them had bleeding faces; one cradled a broken arm. They were walking slowly, limping. There had been a battle somewhere, but we couldn't tell where.

When we reached Changan Avenue, the main east-west thoroughfare, it was full of people as in the days of the great demonstrations – a human river of demonstrators. We followed the flow of it to the Gate of Heavenly Peace, under the bland, moonlike portrait of Chairman Mao. There were hundreds of small groups, each concentrated around someone who was haranguing or lecturing the others, using the familiar, heavy public gestures of the Chinese.

For the most part these were not students. They were from the factories, and the red cloths tied around their heads made them look aggressive, even piratical. Trucks started arriving from the outskirts of the city, full of more young workers, waving the banners of their factories, singing, chanting, looking forward to trouble.

We pushed our way towards the Square where, despite the rumours and the panic, we saw something very different: several thousand people standing in silence, motionless, listening to a large loudspeaker, bolted to a street lamp:

'Go home and save your life. You will fail. You are not behaving in the correct Chinese manner. This is not the West, it is China. You should behave like a good Chinese. Go home and save your life. Go home and save your life.'

The voice was expressionless, epicene,[1] metallic, like that of a hypnotist. I looked at these silent, serious faces, illuminated by the orange light of the street lamps, studying the loudspeaker. Even the small children, brought there with the rest of the family, stared intently. The order was repeated again and again. It was a voice the people of China had been listening to for forty years, and continued listening to even now. But now no one did what the hypnotist said. No one moved.

And then, suddenly, everything changed: the loudspeaker's spell was broken by shouts that the army was coming. There was the sound of a violent scraping, and across the Avenue I saw people pulling at the railings that ran along the roadway and dragging them across the pavement to build a barricade. Everyone moved quickly, a crowd suddenly animated, its actions fast and decisive, sometimes brutal. They blocked off Changan Avenue and the Square itself, and we began filming. People danced around us, flaunting their weaponry: coshes,[2] knives, crude spears, bricks. A boy rushed up to our camera and opened his shabby green wind-cheater to reveal a row of Coca-Cola bottles strapped to his waist, filled with petrol and plugged with rags.

There were very few foreign journalists left in the Square by now, and I felt especially conspicuous. But I also felt good. People grabbed my hand, thanking me for being with them. There was still a spirit of celebration, that they were out on the streets, defying the government, but the spirit was also giving way to a terrible foreboding. There was also something else. Something I hadn't seen before: a reckless ferocity of purpose.

I crossed back into the main part of Tiananmen Square, the village of student tents. There were sticks and cardboard and broken glass underfoot. A student asked me to sign his T-shirt, a craze from earlier days.

'It will be dangerous tonight,' he said. 'We are all very afraid here.'

I finished signing his shirt. I asked him what he thought would happen. 'We will all die.'

He shook my hand again, and slipped away between the tents.

---

[1] *epicene:* neither male nor female
[2] *coshes:* blunt weapons

The camp was dark. There were a few students left; most of them had gathered in the centre of the Square, around the Monument to the People's Heroes. I could hear their speeches and the occasional burst of singing – the Internationale[3] as always. Here, though, it was quiet. This was where the students had chosen to build their statue of the Goddess of Democracy, with her sightless eyes, her torch held in both hands. The symbol of all our aspirations, one of the student leaders called her: the fruit of our struggle. To me, she looked very fragile.

The speeches and the songs continued in the distance. Then suddenly they stopped. There was a violent grinding and a squealing sound – the familiar sound of an armoured personnel carrier. I heard screaming, and behind me, in the Avenue, everyone started running. When I finally spotted the vehicle, I could see that it was making its way with speed down the side of the Square. It seemed uncertain of its direction – one moment driving straight for the Square, and then stopping, turning, stopping again, as if looking for a way to escape. There was a sudden angry roar, and I know it was because the vehicle had crushed someone under its tracks.

The vehicle carried on, careering back and forth. It must have knocked down six or seven people. By now it was on fire, having been hit repeatedly by Molotov cocktails.[4] Somehow, though, it escaped and headed off to the west.

Then a second armoured personnel carrier came along Changan Avenue, alone and unsupported like the first. This time everyone turned and ran hard towards the vehicle, knowing that they, with their numbers and their petrol bombs, had the power to knock it out. They screamed with anger and hate as the vehicle swung randomly in different directions, threatening to knock people down as it made its way through the Square. The Molotov cocktails arched above our heads, spinning over and over, exploding on the thin shell of armour that protected the men inside. Still the vehicle carried on, zigzagging, crossing the Avenue, trying to find a

---

[3] **Internationale:** revolutionary song

[4] **Molotov cocktails:** home made bombs

way through the barricade. A pause, and it charged, head-on, straight into a block of concrete – and then stuck, its engine whirring wildly. A terrible shout of triumph came from the crowd: primitive and dark, its prey finally caught. The smell of petrol and burning metal and sweat was in the air, intoxicating and violent. Everyone around me was pushing and fighting to get to the vehicle. All around me the men seemed to be yelling at the sky, their faces lit up; the vehicle had caught fire. A man – his torso bare – climbed up the side of the vehicle and stood on top of it, his arms raised in victory, the noise of the mob welling up around him. They knew they had the vehicle's crew trapped inside. Someone started beating at the armoured glass with an iron bar.

The screaming around me rose even louder; the handle of the door at the rear of the vehicle had turned a little, and the door began to open. A soldier pushed the barrel of a gun out, but it was snatched from his hands, and then everyone started grabbing his arms, pulling and wrenching until finally he came free and then he was gone: I saw the arms of the mob, flailing, raised above their heads as they fought to get their blows in. He was dead within seconds, and his body was dragged away in triumph. A second soldier showed his head through the door and was then immediately pulled out by his hair and ears and the skin on his face. This soldier's eyes were rolling, and his mouth was open and he was covered with blood where the skin had been ripped off. Only his eyes remained – white and clear – but then someone was trying to get them as well, and someone else began beating his skull until the skull came apart, and there was blood all over the ground, and his brains, and still they kept on beating and beating what was left.

Then the horrible sight passed away, and the ground was wet where he had been.

The vehicle burned for a long time, its driver and the man beside him burning with it. The flames lit up the Square and reflected on the face of the Monument where the students had taken their stand. The crowd in Changan Avenue had been sated. The loudspeakers had stopped telling people to save their lives. There was silence.

The students sang the Internationale. It would be for the last time, and it sounded weak and faint in the vastness of the Square. Many were crying. No doubt some students joined in the attacks on the army, but those in the Square kept to their principle of nonviolence. Although the army suffered the first casualties, it was the students who would be the martyrs that night.

My colleagues and I wanted to save our pictures in case we were arrested. We took up our position on the fourteenth floor of the Beijing Hotel. From there, everything seemed grey and distant. We saw most of what happened, but we were separated from the fear and the noise and the stench of it. We saw the troops pouring out of the Gate of Heavenly Peace, bayonets fixed, shooting first into the air and then straight ahead of them. They looked like automata,[5] with their rounded dark helmets. We filmed them charging across and clearing the northern end of the Square, where I had signed the student's T-shirt. We filmed the tanks as they drove over the tents where some of the students had taken refuge. We filmed as the lights in the Square were switched off at 4 am. They were switched on again forty minutes later, when the troops and the tanks moved towards the Monument itself, shooting first in the air and then, again, directly at the students themselves, so that the steps of the Monument and the heroic reliefs which decorated it were smashed by bullets.

I had seen the river of protest running along Changan Avenue; I had seen a million people in the streets, demanding a way of life that was better than rule by corruption and secret police. I recalled the lines of the T'ang dynasty poet Li Po, that if you cut water with a sword you merely made it run faster. But the river of change had been dammed, and below me, in the Avenue where it had run, people were dying. Beside me, the cameraman spotted something and started filming. Down in the Square, in the early light, the soldiers were busy unrolling something and lifting it up. Soon a great curtain of black cloth covered the entrance to Tiananmen Square. What was happening there was hidden from us.

---

[5] **automata:** robots

Protests in Argentina

Miranda France

Different governments react differently to criticism of their regimes. In 1993 Miranda France, a young freelance journalist, arrived in Argentina. In her book Bad Times in Buenos Aires *she tries to make sense of the strange things that happened to her there. Unlike the Chinese government, the Argentinian authorities seemed positively to encourage demonstrations and protests.*

'Your problem,' said Raquel, 'is that you try to see Argentina as a normal country. It's abnormal. It's a country that doesn't work.'

There was, at least, a freedom to complain. Demonstrations were frequent, fervent, and sometimes the whole city was encouraged to take part in them, with radio announcements and scattered leaflets urging a mass show of solidarity at an appointed hour. One evening, thousands of *porteños*[1] appeared on their balconies, banging saucepans with wooden spoons to protest against government corruption; another time they kept a minute's silence in memory of a murdered journalist. When the cost of local calls doubled, people boycotted the telephone for a fixed number of hours a day. With so many protests, it was hard to remember when to keep silent and when to be noisy, when to light candles and when to boycott the telephone – assuming it was working.

On Thursday afternoons, the Mothers of the Disappeared held a vigil in front of the president's palace in the Plaza de Mayo, to protest the continuing freedom of their children's killers. On Wednesdays it was the turn of a more violent and noisy faction: the elderly. Under the new economic regime, pensioners had lost almost all entitlement to state benefits – their money had simply evaporated during the days of hyperinflation ... On Wednesday afternoons, thousands of pensioners held an enraged demonstration outside the Congress, which was liable to end in a riot. They were a bizarre sight, these geriatric hooligans,

---

[1] ***porteños:*** inhabitants of Buenos Aires

rattling crash barriers and spraying graffiti; one old man could do a trick with his false teeth for the cameras. Once, during a protest, a septuagenarian[2] activist had her wig stolen by a rival group of pensioners. Infuriated, she ran squawking through the streets around the Congress. Her legs swathed in support bandages, her earrings an obscene adornment to her baldness, she looked remarkably like a dodo.[3]

The rhythmic beating of a bombo drum,[4] signalling another protest, became a peculiarly violent sound to my ears. I would go down and stand on the front balcony as the people streamed underneath, a dizzying turbulence of banners, fliers and colours. There were protests against corruption in politics and the law courts, against the government's economic policy and university underfunding. On the anniversary of the Falklands War, a noisy procession of veterans made its way to the war monument, vowing to return and recapture the islands.

Once, coming out of a back street on to our avenue, I found myself swept into a Peronist rally campaigning for the re-election of the president. The noise and movement were tremendous; the demonstrators blew whistles and waved Argentine flags and there was the violent thrashing of the drum again, very loud this time, because I was right beside it. The drummer's face, red from exertion and pouring sweat, was a picture of derangement; his features seemed contorted by a painful ecstasy. He was beating the drum with such a frenzy that he had scraped his knuckles raw, and the parchment was streaming with blood. Yet still he went on, bashing the bleeding hand against the drum. I thought the man was crazed in the pursuit of politics; either that, or he was a slave to the drum. In any case, I could never forget him. A long time afterwards, when I was living in London, the rhythmic banging of bass-heavy music from a passing car could still induce in me a momentary anxiety I recognised from those times. For a few seconds I could feel transported to the streets of Buenos Aires.

---

[2] **septuagenarian:** seventy-year-old
[3] **dodo:** extinct bird
[4] **bombo-drum:** bass drum

The Crowd Went Wild

Jack Pizzey

If you want to learn to dance the samba in Rio de Janiero, you go to a samba school. Here Jack Pizzey describes two rival samba schools, each intent on winning the competition for the best display in the annual carnival. Beija Flor (all white, in identical blue and white costumes) is financed by a rich white man Pizzey calls The Entrepreneur. Mangueira (predominantly black; anything goes as long as it is pink and green) is led by beautiful Cledilce from the favela (shanty town) and funded mainly by illegal lotteries. The contest between the two schools becomes a duel between processed cheese and raw sugar, white and black, rich and poor.

The start time of the *carnaval* had been scheduled – as usual – for five. It began six hours late, at eleven. As usual.

It was three hours later, at two in the morning, that Beija Flor and The Entrepreneur's turn came. And by the time Mangueira got the order to launch themselves down the avenue past the grandstands, the sun was already up. Beija Flor had been magnificent: their floats had been impeccable and lavish; their blue and white thousands of dancers had moved as one with the precision of guardsmen; after a slight hitch in getting his float under a bridge, The Entrepreneur had stood suavely elegant, anticipating victory. Cledilce and Mangueira could not hope to match that polish. Before Mangueira was half an hour into its parade, Cledilce had grown so excited that her discipline was gone. She broke the ranks to dance an exuberant solo and was smacked back into line by the School's white-haired president. But the crowd was enjoying it. They'd been in their seats since the afternoon of the day before, their eyes were heavy in the early morning light, but Mangueira was beginning to rouse them. The drums pounded, three thousand shimmering dancers sang and kicked and waved, lifting the audience gradually to its feet to wave and sing back.

More and more people jumped to their feet, higher-pitched drums cut in to raise the temperature again and again until the dawn was jumping with thirty thousand people on their feet, hands high and crooning Mangueira's song. Below the stamping audience Mangueira's ranks of black mamas swirled, eyes and teeth shining beneath pink and green head scarves; dancers now sashayed freely out of the ranks to dance their raw sugar message: vitality, earthiness, laughter, exuberance. They were the people from the *favelas* and this was *their* day.

They eclipsed all who had gone before. It was another hour before they'd danced their way to the end of the grandstands, and by then such was the enthusiasm of the crowds that Mangueira's President decided to break all the rules and take the School right back up the avenue again and invite the audience to climb down from the stands and join them. The sun rose higher, Cledilce wept tears of jubilation, the audience flowed down to mix with the pink and green, the drums whacked out a victorious crescendo. There was no doubt: the old vitality of the *favela* had triumphed over the sophistication of the smart set. Raw sugar had beaten processed cheese. It was the hour of Mangueira. They were kings-for-a-day. At the end of the avenue the crowd, now bearing the three thousand pink and green dancers along, began to melt away towards buses, taxis, lunch. Soon the kings would be back in the *favelas* and it would be just another day.

Activities

Understanding
Disaster at Hillsborough
1 What are the main differences between the crowds at Heysel and at Hillsborough? Why do you think David Miller points out these differences?
2 What was the initial reaction to the disaster from the Nottingham Forest supporters?
3 What were the main reasons for what might, in other circumstances, have been unnecessary deaths?

Tiananmen Square
4 Explain as fully as you can why the crowd was pleased that John Simpson stayed in the Square.
5 Why do you think Simpson ends his report with the description of a black curtain being put up across the entrance to Tiananmen Square? In what ways is it appropriate?

Protests in Argentina
6 List some of the protests that have taken place in Argentina.
7 Do you agree with the quotation from Raquel that begins this extract?
8 In what ways is Argentina described as abnormal?

The Crowd Went Wild
9 Describe how the feelings of the crowd change during this extract.

Style
Disaster at Hillsborough
10 David Miller makes repeated use of the phrase 'We watched them die'. How does his use of this phrase help to convey a sense of his frustration and helplessness?
11 This extract uses plenty of short paragraphs and includes information from a variety of sources. How does this affect our understanding of the tragedy and how we respond to it?

Tiananmen Square
12 John Simpson only uses direct quotation occasionally. Find three examples and comment on why he has included these words.
13 Find examples of the times Simpson describes the crowd as if it were a single creature. How does this help us to understand some of the behaviour he observed?

Protests in Argentina

14 How does Miranda France characterise the different crowds she encountered? What is the general tone of her piece?

15 How does France use drums to link her narrative together in this extract?

The Crowd Went Wild

16 Look carefully at Jack Pizzey's use of sentences in this account. Find an example of a very short sentence and an example of a long one and explain why you think each is used effectively.

Speaking and listening

17 🗩 Do you think mass protests are a good way of expressing political opinions? Discuss some of the protests that have happened recently – did they have an effect on public opinion?

Comparisons

18 Being in a large excited crowd can often be very confusing. How do the authors in this section create a sense of the moods and movements of the crowds?

19 'Disaster at Hillsborough' is a reflective eyewitness report whereas 'Tiananmen Square' tries to give an impression of events as they happened. How do the two authors structure their accounts to create the impressions they want?

20 'Protests in Argentina' and 'The Crowd Went Wild' are both light-hearted in tone. Compare and contrast the way the two extracts achieve their moods.

Further activity

21 Have you ever been in a large crowd? Write a brief account of your experiences and try to give an impression of the crowd's purpose, behaviour and mood.

🗩 Speaking and listening work

Acknowledgements

The publishers gratefully acknowledge the following for permission to reproduce copyright material. Every effort has been made to trace copyright holders, but in some cases has proved impossible. The publishers would be happy to hear from any copyright holder that has not been acknowledged.

The Fall of President Marcos by James Fenton, published by Granta Publications Limited. Copyright © James Fenton 1986. Reprinted by permission of Peters, Fraser & Dunlop on behalf of James Fenton

'War Games' by Grace Bradberry, from *The Times* 12 August 2000. Copyright © Times Newspapers Limited, 12 August 2000, and 'Good Evening, Liberated Serbia' by Misha Glenny, from *The Times* 6 October 2000. Copyright © Times Newspapers Limited. Reprinted by permission

Leaves from the Journal of Our Life in the Highlands from 1848–1861 Queen Victoria, edited by Arthur Helps. Reprinted by permission of the Folio Society Limited

The Life and Death of Thomas Beckett by William Fitzstephen. Copyright © 1961 The Folio Society Limited. Reprinted with permission of the Folio Society Limited

The Jubilee Year by Roger Hudson. Copyright © 1996 The Folio Society Limited. Reprinted with permission of the Folio Society Limited

Hard Times by Studs Terkel. Copyright © Studs Terkel. Reprinted by permission of International Creative Management, Inc.

Out of Order by Frank Johnson, published by Robson Books in 1982. Copyright © 1982 by Frank Johnson. Reprinted by permission of the publishers

In Xanadu – A Quest by William Dalrymple, published by HarperCollins*Publishers*. Reprinted by permission of the publishers

A Fleet of Being by Rudyard Kipling. Reprinted by permission of A.P. Watt Limited on behalf of the National Trust for Places of Historical Interest or Natural Beauty

My Early Life by Winston Churchill. Copyright Winston S. Churchill. Reprinted by permission of Curtis Brown Limited, London on behalf of the Estate of Sir Winston S. Churchill